WINDOW TREATMENTS
IDEA BOOK

SUE SAMPSON AND ELLEN DELUCIA

The Taunton Press

The Taunton Press
Inspiration for hands-on living®

The Taunton Press, Inc., 63 South Main Street, PO Box 5506, Newtown, CT 06470-5506
e-mail: tp@taunton.com

Editor: Jennifer Peters
Interior Design and Layout: David Giammattei
Illustrator: Christine Erickson
Front cover photographers: (top row, left to right) © Jessie Walker, © Sandy Agrafiotis,
© Tim Street-Porter, © Tim Street-Porter; (middle row, left to right) © Eric Roth,
© Melabee M. Miller, © Nancy Hill, © Alise O'Brien; (bottow row, left to right)
© Brian Vanden Brink, © Nancy Hill, © Samu Studios, © Chipper Hatter.
Back cover photographers: (top) © Mark Lohman; (bottom, left to right) © Barry Halkin,
© Mark Lohman, © Roger Turk; (author photo) © Mike LaChioma.

Library of Congress Cataloging-in-Publication Data

Sampson, Sue.
  Window treatments idea book : design ideas, fabric & color, embellishing ready-made,
measuring & installing, tips for instant style /cSue Sampson and Ellen DeLucia.
     p. cm.
  Includes bibliographical references and index.
  ISBN-13: 978-1-56158-819-0 (alk. paper)
  ISBN-10: 1-56158-819-9 (alk. paper)
  1. Draperies. 2. Window shades. 3. Windows in interior decoration. 4. Valances (Windows)
  5. Cornices. I. DeLucia, Ellen. II. Title.
  TT390.S26 2006
  747'.3–dc22
                              2005033432

Printed in China
10 9 8 7 6 5 4 3

Acknowledgments

Our thanks begin with McCall Pattern Company, where our Home Dec in A Sec® sewing patterns were launched. Many thanks to Tony Devino, Carol Garey, James Bosco, Dianna Murphy, and Brian Kraus for their creative photography talents; Kathy Lenn, Nancy DiCocco, and Joy McKeon for their keen marketing insight; Joe Enslemo and Gail Hamilton for help with licensing and public relations; Valerie Zeis and the Fabric Library crew who always help us find just the right fabrics, and to Hank Miller for being kind when our guide-sheets are a tad too long.

Heartfelt thanks also go to the talented Taunton group—to Maria Taylor for giving us this opportunity, Carolyn Mandarano for her expert wisdom and thoughtful manner, Jenny Peters for her editing wizardry, Julie Hamilton for her organizational skills, and Wendi Mijal for her photography expertise. Thank you also to Nancy Hill, who spent a day with us in the sweltering heat photographing windows, and to the many photographers whose gorgeous work fills these pages.

Special thanks from Sue: A big thank you to Robin Sanders, for beginning my career, to Sanna Brown and Dot Reutlinger who really did teach me how to sew, and to Madeline Walrod for her support long ago. Nothing would be possible without the encouragement of my very patient and wonderful husband Paul, and two other "best buds"—Mom and Wendy. And love and thanks to my terrific girls—Katie, Dana, and Brittany, who put up with hearing "I'll be there in a minute" too many times. Special thanks from Ellen: I wish to thank my Mom for teaching me the joy of sewing and to my friend and neighbor Sue for expanding on that knowledge. To my husband Ernie, my best friend and partner for life, and our three great kids, Jenny, Annie, and Ernie, who can always make me smile; thanks for your love and support.

We would also like to thank all of the people we've spoken to over the years who have enjoyed sewing with our patterns and browsing the website—you continue to inspire us!

Contents

Introduction

Congratulations! By picking up this book you've taken a giant step toward creating the windows of your dreams. Maybe you've collected countless fabric swatches in your search for the right window treatments, yet somehow can't make a final decision on what will look best. Or perhaps you have a cherished fabric but are hesitant about the style of window décor that will suit your needs. If you've just purchased a new home, figuring out how to decorate the windows can be a daunting task. Whatever your reasons are for living with undecorated windows, you are not alone. Most people would rather live with bare windows than risk a less-than-perfect selection!

Why take the risk? Because window treatments can make us feel good. The right combination of style and fabric adorning a window has the ability to comfort and soothe us after a long, hectic day. Simply put, window treatments are the design element that can transform a room from cold and uninviting to warm and welcoming—the kind of place you'd like to spend time in, to relax on the couch, sip a cup of tea, and enjoy the latest novel. Your home is where memories are created, where you live some of your best moments with family and friends.

It's understandable if you're not sure where to begin. A simple trip to the fabric store can be like opening Pandora's box, with an overwhelming number of fabric, trim, and window treatment style choices. But rest assured, the process of selecting just the right style and fabric for your win-dow is within your reach. Whether you're in the do-it-yourself or do-it-for-me mode, all you need is a little know-how and a touch of confidence. Within these pages, you'll find the information and resources you need to create stunning windows, whether you're updating an existing space or starting from scratch in a newly constructed home or addition.

We've helped thousands of people make just the right choice for window décor with our McCall's® Home Dec In A Sec sewing pattern line and our interactive Web site for custom window treatments, www.HomeDecInASec.com. This book was designed just for you—because we understand the value you place on how your home looks and feels. We understand what it's like to juggle busy work lives with family and community commitments. Despite time constraints, we still find moments to decorate our homes so we have a comfortable place to land at the end of the day. We hope to help you enjoy the window decorating process as much as we do, so let's get started together.

Room Index

Selecting Window Treatments

Windows are one of the most significant design elements in a home—not just in grand rooms with soaring floor-to-ceiling windows, but in every room no matter how big and spacious or small and unassuming the space. Windows are the openings to the world, allowing natural light in while providing access to a beautiful view, a glimpse of moonlight, or a wonderful breeze. But deciding how to decorate a window can be a daunting task, especially since there are so many questions to consider. What window treatment style will suit your needs best? How can you make the most of a custom window? How much will it all cost? Which fabric should you choose—print, solid, texture, sheer? And most important, will you be happy with the window treatments you select?

No worries. That is the simple answer to all of the questions above. The journey begins with knowledge, and this chapter will guide you through the decision-making process by providing key pieces of information to consider. Once the basic questions are answered, the fun of selecting the right window treatment styles to reflect your personality and lifestyle begins.

◄ IN REMODELED OR NEWLY CONSTRUCTED HOMES, many homeowners are opting for arch-top windows that call for creative non-traditional window treatment styling. Cleverly designed panels form a soft backdrop in this room, while the navy rings draw attention to the beautiful lines of the windows.

What's Your Decorating Style?

EVERYONE HAS A DECORATING STYLE, and finding your own is easy. Begin by looking in your closet. There you'll find the colors you gravitate toward and the fashion designs you prefer. Tailored styles of clothing often equate to traditional themes in decorating. Whimsical, free-spirited fashions indicate you might prefer a more relaxed, creative approach to home décor. Reinforce your findings by flipping through decorating books and magazines to create a file of your favorite room settings. You'll see a theme emerging in the furnishings, wall colors, fabrics, and window treatment styles you favor. Remember, home is where you live your life. By creating surroundings based on your personal tastes and preferences, you'll find a sense of serenity every time you walk through the door.

▲ AN ORDINARY CORNER is transformed into a delightful writing nook with a graceful valance mounted just below the ceiling. Side panels in matching fabric flow onto the floor—a look that breaks tradition and adds softness to the setting.

NEW TRADITIONAL

Traditional with a twist best describes this new style of classic decorating. If you favor traditional styles, you would feel at home with a mix of antique or quality reproduction furnishings, vintage china and crystal, and sterling silver accents. Your rooms could have touches of your personal heritage, such as a framed collection of old photographs or a delicate secretary desk inherited from a loved one. New traditional styling combines the past with the present by infusing spontaneity into formalized settings with textures and colors. Just as a wrought iron coffee table can coexist gracefully with a Queen Anne chair, stunning striped silk drapery panels in vivid hues can be complemented with a soft cornice on top. The key is to create settings with welcoming elegance, where rooms are still family-friendly places to enjoy meals and conversation together.

▶ LUXURIOUSLY FULL PANELS give warmth to these large windows while serving as a backdrop for the traditional-style furnishings. The red border on the draperies along with the unique coffee table, pillows, and accessories add spontaneity to the formal setting.

▲ A MIX OF FUN AND FORMALITY sets the tone in this dining room. The elegance of the crystal chandelier, rich wood tones, and melon-colored damask couch is mimicked with a playful striped silk adorning the windows. The fabric is showcased across the soft cornice with trim that follows the gently scalloped edges.

RETRO INSPIRED

If retro is your passion, you take pleasure in furnishings and accents reminiscent of things past. You are likely to enjoy spending time scouring flea markets and tag sales for vintage pieces. A carefully planned collection of furniture in distressed woods or crackled patinas would make you happy, and broken-in leather would be a first choice for a new chair. The lines in retro-inspired rooms are clean and simple with a range of wall colors from simple whites to vivid, offbeat tones such as a golden yellow or apple green. Simplicity is paramount when it comes to selecting window dressings for the retro style, allowing the interesting mix of furnishings to shine.

▶ THE LIVELY YELLOW in the faux-painted walls draws attention to the interesting mix of retro-inspired furnishings. Plaid drapery panels are mounted on a black iron rod, an accent color that is repeated throughout the room. Treating the bay window with shutters keeps the look simple.

▶ THE TAILORED WHITE BALLOON valances purposely fade into this hallway setting. The treatment style adds dimensional interest without overpowering the collection of treasures.

Where to Start

Whether you're starting a decorating project from scratch or are updating existing rooms, begin with a simple strategy.

1. Start with something you love—a couch, rug, wall color, painting, or fabric. Pick one item and work your color and decorating scheme around it.

2. If you're redecorating, eliminate the items you don't care for. It doesn't make sense to restyle a room around a couch that you've been unhappy with for years.

3. Look for a room that inspires you to imitate. Visualizing how a finished room will look is difficult so it's best to peruse magazines, watch home shows, and visit local show houses and model homes.

4. Team up with a friend who has a sense of style that matches yours. Or, look into hiring a design consultant to select a wall color or help you put a plan together. This may save you money in the end.

▼ A DISTRESSED MIRROR, slipcovered chairs, and lamp make a statement in this '50s-style retro-inspired living room. Woven wood roll-up shades, reminiscent of bamboo shades from years ago, provide simple styling and function on the windows.

COUNTRY CHIC

Today's country is a combination of styles, where Old World European meets New Age with a unique mix of fabrics, furnishings, and decorative touches. Country chic rooms can be dressed up in sophisticated splendor with accents such as beautiful English toile fabrics that grace a couch or form romantic balloon shades, yet they also often contain contrasting features like a rustic coffee table or a polished wood mirror. A more relaxed country look occurs when comfortable gathering spaces include an interesting mixture of wood shades and furniture styles. A wicker chair looks at home alongside a traditionally styled couch, and weathered pine pieces appear in perfect harmony next to those made from bamboo. You may find bold checks and plaids used as accents on pillows or as focal points on the window or couch. Window décor is integral to the overall country chic feel, and treatment styling is often traditional, with fabric print or texture playing the main role.

▲ BUSY TILE COUNTERTOPS and backsplashes call for a simple style at the window. A straight, gathered valance in a mini-print fabric provides just the right touch, and the 10-in. depth allows plenty of light to flow through the windows.

▼ MATCHSTICK-STYLE WOVEN SHADES complement the interesting mix of woods in this relaxed country chic room. The shades were cleverly made in two parts—one covers the top transom window and a second shade covers the area below. The filtered daylight provides a cooling touch to this sunny setting.

◄ WHITE WAS SELECTED as the predominant color for this elegant country living room, allowing the rug, fabrics, pillows, and accessories to take center stage. The simple styling of the drapery panels is enhanced with beautiful tassel trim that cascades down the leading edges.

Working Around Existing Features

The most cost-efficient way to update a bathroom is to work a decorating scheme around existing tile, countertops, and cabinetry. Start by selecting a fabric that complements the tile. It may be hard to find an exact match for the old tile color, so it's best to concentrate on finding a fabric that blends well. Try painting old cabinets white and adding new knobs, making fabric skirts to hide unsightly openings or radiators, and installing new lighting fixtures. Paint or paper the walls to draw attention away from dated features. Your finishing touch can be installing window treatments with interesting details such as pleats, contrasting inserts, bandings, and trims to help accentuate the most redeeming features in the room—the windows.

► DATED TILE AND CABINETRY in this older bathroom were revamped with new life when blue toile balloon shades were mounted high above a set of narrow windows. The decorative banding and striped fabric peeking through the shade pleats draw attention away from the counter area. The matching wallpaper makes the room appear larger than it is.

METRO MODERN

A distinctive style that works equally well in an urban apartment or country manor, the metro modern style consists of unique lines and slick décor. If your tastes lean toward metro, you might enjoy a neutral color scheme that highlights the shape of the furniture or dramatic color of a pillow or rug. Accents within the room would feature highly polished surfaces that gleam, contrasted by striking objects such as a uniquely shaped nickel coffee table or hand-hewn pottery urn. You'll often find black or eye-popping primary colors used sparingly in the room, lending an element of surprise that plays off the white or neutral-tone walls. Drapery panels at the window suit this style, especially if the fabric features texture or interest, such as a unique stenciled border along the bottom edge.

▲ THE VARIOUS TEXTURES and surfaces of the wall tiles create a contemporary feel in this room, and the theme remains consistent with the uniquely shaped coffee tables and sofas. A subtle white drapery panel is tied back on the two-story wall, bringing warmth to windows that would otherwise appear stark.

▼ WHILE SHEER DRAPES are traditionally white, a charcoal gray was selected here to provide an interesting backdrop for the sleek setting. The translucent quality of the fabric allows a filtered view of the magnificent skyline.

Decorating with Panels

Panels are the most popular choice of all window treatment styles for multiple reasons. Framing a window in fabric evokes feelings of hospitality, security, and comfort in a room, while providing decorative appeal and functionality. Panels also have a disguising element—they can make windows appear wider or taller or both, and sheer panels can filter out an unsightly view. Pleated headings along the top of drapes are fashionable picks while traditionally gathered panels create lovely effects, especially when the panels remain stationary at the sides of the window. When selecting a fabric, remember that draperies that blend with the walls will fade into the setting, while bold, contrasting panels will become immediate focal points.

▶ RICH VELVET PANELS create column-like effects and provide startling contrast to the neutral tones of this room's furnishings. The silky texture of the box-stitched bed covering and pillows adds touches of luxury to the room.

▶ THE CLEAN LINES of this metro-inspired room are pleasantly interrupted with the stimulating shapes of the end table and the massive urn behind the seating area. Floor-to-ceiling drapery panels unite the windows, and the black leafy stenciling provides interest.

CREATIVE HARMONY

In a room that features creative harmony, you may see a variety of fabrics, furnishings, and accessories that work together in artistic ways. Everything in the space is chosen with a discerning eye, and there is often a surprising fabric print or unusual combination of decorative items that add a spark to the room. If you like creative harmony, you probably enjoy art in all forms and prefer a mix of different wood finishes and furnishing styles—the less traditionally matched, the better. An elegant couch with an assortment of interesting pillows in various prints, colors, and textures would be harmoniously paired with flea market finds such as a rattan chair or an end table with an iron base. The creative flair extends to the windows, too, with striking fabrics fashioned into distinctively designed window coverings.

▲ A LEOPARD PRINT makes a big splash in this bathroom, especially when it's used on the window and in the shower. The fabric print forms a creative border along the sides of the shade. The effect starts at the ceiling, where the shade and curtain are mounted for room-heightening drama.

▶ RAINBOW-INSPIRED STRIPES form a cascading focal point in this creatively designed living room. Artistic touches are found throughout the area, from the playful tassel trim running along the lower edge of the couch to the eclectic assortment of colorful pillows. The window treatment provides unity, tying all the colors together.

Designing with Borders

There are many ways to create an interesting border effect on a panel. Border print fabrics, where the print runs along the lengthwise edge of the fabric, can be positioned so that the decorative edge is highlighted across a valance or down the length of a drapery panel. If you go this route, select a border print featuring an all-over design that looks the same when viewed from all directions to ensure that the print looks the same whether it's placed horizontally or vertically. Another way to create a border effect is to stitch bands of contrast fabric along the edges of a window treatment. Be sure the finished bands are at least 2 in. wide so they will be noticeable from across the room.

▲ AN APPEALING MIX of fabrics and mementos makes this window nook cozy. The bold wallpaper print inspired the homeowner to use bordered panels that feature wide fabric bands made from a coordinating print.

◄ FABRICS FEATURING BORDERS as part of the print can be engineered so that the border falls along the bottom of a valance or down the leading edges of drapery panels as was done here. Enhancing the edges with a lengthy tassel trim adds another well-crafted touch.

Find Your Window Type

DETERMINING WHICH WINDOW TREATMENT designs will work best for your room depends on the style of the windows. First, take into account how the window opens. The treatment should not interfere with a window that cranks open into the room or tilts in for cleaning purposes. It's also helpful to know what kind of window you have. Standard windows, often coupled or grouped in threes, are what most people have in their homes.

In new or remodeled homes, specialty windows, with their beautiful architectural lines that draw attention, are more prevalent. Specialty windows include arch-top and Palladian types, known for their elegantly curved shape, sometimes accompanied by transom windows featuring a distinctive top row of rectangular windows. When treating specialty windows keep in mind that the window covering should complement, not detract from, the inherent beauty of the window. No matter what your window type, the key to success in selecting the right window treatment style is to enhance the window, whether it is new and grand or classic and modest.

▲ DOUBLE-HUNG WINDOWS positioned next to a transom door present a decorating dilemma. This solution combines cellular shades for privacy and a valance across all to unify the windows with the door.

STANDARD WINDOWS

DOUBLE HUNG

CASEMENT

PICTURE

JALOUSIE

AWNING

While there are many kinds of standard windows, these are the five most common.

DOUBLE HUNG: This window type features two glass units called sashes that slide up and down. Mullions, the grids or slats that divide the glass, are often featured on double-hung and casement windows.

CASEMENT: This window is generally hinged at the side or bottom and can be made up of gliding sash units that open to the side.

PICTURE: To maximize the view, these windows are comprised of one large expanse of glass that does not open, usually flanked by two side windows.

JALOUSIE: A porch-style window found in older homes made up of a series of horizontal glass slats that tilt open.

AWNING: Hinged at the top or the bottom, an awning window cranks or pushes out.

▲ THESE CLASSIC DOUBLE-HUNG WINDOWS are appropriately styled with a classic style window treatment. To enhance the clean lines of the setting, the Roman shades were mounted inside each window, providing vertical movement that visually elongates the windows.

STANDARD WINDOWS

Decorating standard-style windows is relatively easy since they are rectangular and there are no curves to navigate. However, it's important to begin by assessing all of the windows within the room. While some rooms contain identical windows, it's more common for rooms to feature a variety of types and sizes. For example, a room may include a picture window at one end, multiple double-hung windows, and a sliding door, all on different walls. Special considerations may affect the style of treatment you choose, such as windows in corners or installed at differing heights on the wall. Your goal is to unify the room with the same fabric on each window and door unit, and to mount treatments at the same heights, if possible, to create consistency and balance throughout the setting.

▼ THE EASIEST DECORATING scenario occurs when a room features multiple single windows with ample wall space around each. Mounting drapery panels on the wall and at ceiling height allows windows to appear grander in scale.

Traditional Windows

Standard double-hung windows are most commonly featured as single units, but they can also be found grouped together in a corner bump-out or as double or triple windows framed with distinctive moldings. Multiple windows can be dressed individually or as one window.

▲ A SINGLE CASEMENT WINDOW is the focal point of this inviting dining nook. The scalloped edge of the valance is highlighted with a decorative braid and buttons, helping to soften the angular lines of the room. For added privacy, a woven-wood shade has been installed inside the window frame.

▲ TWO TRADITIONAL WINDOWS, placed side by side, are treated with softly folded fabric shades highlighting a noteworthy print design. Mounting the shades inside the window frame brings focus to the interesting trim work, painted to match the kitchen cabinets.

▲ THIS EATING AREA is surrounded by individual windows that are tied together with a softly gathered balloon valance. Mounting the treatments at ceiling height allows maximum light to enter the room and capitalizes on the view of the backyard.

ARCH-TOP AND TRANSOM WINDOWS

If you have recently completed a renovation or purchased a new home, chances are you have a few specialty windows that give a unique architectural element to your home. While striking to look at, arch-top and transom windows provide a challenge in selecting the right window treatment that offers both beauty and function. Arch-top windows, with their sweeping curves, and transom windows let in excessive light, causing glare and possible harm to textiles, artwork, and wood furnishings in the room. In addition, a large window can create black hole effect when the sun goes down. All of these things should be considered when selecting a proper window treatment.

▶ THIS ARCH TRANSOM WINDOW was equipped with wood blinds for privacy, but its size made the room appear stark. Drapery panels mounted in line with the top of the arch stack onto the wall, allowing the gracious arch shape to be revealed.

ARCH-TOP AND TRANSOM WINDOWS

SEPARATE ARCH TOP   ONE-PIECE ARCH TOP   PALLADIAN

ARCH TRANSOM   BASIC TRANSOM

Here are some guidelines to follow when treating specialty windows.

SEPARATE ARCH TOP: Window treatments can be placed along the dividing molding between the arch and bottom window or can be made to follow the curve of the arch.

ONE-PIECE ARCH TOP: Since there is no dividing line where the arch begins, window treatments must be placed above the arch or must be made to follow the curve.

PALLADIAN: Treat these windows at the sides or below the arch if there is molding separating the arch top from the lower window.

ARCH TRANSOM: The window can be treated below the transom or above, depending upon the style chosen.

BASIC TRANSOM: The transom can be treated with a separate woven-wood shade or like the arch transom.

▲ **TALL, NARROW WINDOWS** capped with pie-shaped arches give this room unique character but make the windows hard to treat. To create unity among all of the windows, drapery panels were mounted below the arches and at the same height on the window located on the adjacent wall.

VISUALIZING THE STYLES

Finding ways to decorate specialty windows involves a little bit of searching, which fortunately can be done over the Internet. Interactive Web sites allow you to click through the latest window treatment designs and apply decorator fabrics to the picture so you can see exactly how the fabric will appear on a specific style window. If you have a digital camera, there are computer software programs you can use to take a photo of your window and then place window treatment styles directly on the picture. The small investment for software will pay off in the end, especially if you have many windows to decorate.

▲ FORMAL FABRICS LEND an air of grace to a dramatically styled dining room. Stationary side panels are color blocked to accent the wall with cocoa colored damask running along the drape top, purposely ending in line with the transom.

◄ THIS ROOM SHOWS an innovative approach to window treatments by placing woven-wood shades below the transoms, allowing the distinctive lines of the window to show. Unlined drapery panels tacked above the side windows and tied to the side allow additional light to filter through.

Specialty Windows

If you have a house full of windows just waiting for inspiration, the DreamDraper® software program may be the design tool you're looking for. It imports digital photos of your windows and allows you to drop hundreds of window treatment designs directly on the image. Fabric prints and colors can be added to the photo or you can scan in your own decorator fabric. All fabrics and window styles are sized to true scale. Background effects can be added to further simulate your unique room.

◄ THIS HOMEOWNER DESIGNED a gorgeous treatment for her grand-scale Palladian window using the DreamDraper software. The swags and leaf/bird medallions dropped on the photos were selected from the artwork components included with the program.

► CREATING A TRIANGLE VALANCE with long flowing panels allowed the homeowner to visualize the effect of leaving the gracious center window untreated. Many of the design components in the program are replicas of actual products that can be purchased, such as the whimsical drapery rod.

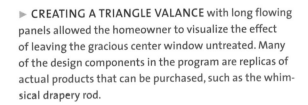

BAY WINDOWS

A bay window always provides a unique dimension and added space to a room, whether the window is a walk-in variety adding square footage or features a shelf used to display favorite keepsakes. Technically, a window is considered a bay when three or more windows are placed at angles to one another on an exterior wall. To design treatments for a bay, begin by determining if you want to unite the windows as one by running a continuous valance across all, or whether you want to frame each window individually with valances, shades, or side panels that are cut to fit each unit. Also, consider where to mount the treatment. Installing window décor at ceiling height within the bay or on the outside wall gives the window a sweeping illusion of loftiness.

▲ THIS BAY-STYLE DINING AREA feels more intimate with the help of drapery panels mounted below the transom windows. The bold border edging the draperies helps to create pleasing focal points within the setting and coordinates with the valance in the adjoining room.

▶ THIS BAY WINDOW is treated in two ways— on the outside wall with drapery panels and on each individual window with woven shades. The panels anchor the ends of the bay by spilling onto the wall, adding width to the window. The shades can be closed for privacy, sheltering occupants from view.

CHALLENGE: Personalizing a Bay Eating Area

A series of four lengthy transom windows within a bay setting made the area feel cold and austere at mealtime. The homeowners were looking for a way to add intimacy without compromising the look of the windows.

SOLUTION: For privacy, the decorator mounted semi-sheer woven shades above the transoms on each individual window. The translucency of the shades still allows the handsome shape of the windows to show through. Drapery panels were then mounted at the sides of each window on wood poles painted to blend in with the molding, allowing the painted tray ceiling to attract attention. The geometric plaid selected for the drapes adds contemporary flair to the casual setting, providing decorative punch without overwhelming the room.

▶ A DECISION TO TREAT all of the windows individually actually brought unity to this bay area. Since there were so many windows, a panoramic effect is still achieved because the drapery panels take up little space, allowing most of the glass to be exposed.

BOW WINDOWS

A bow window sweeps away from the wall like a bay window, providing an expansive display of glass that can showcase a beautiful outdoor vista. The arched quality can dramatically change the angular feel of a room while adding an interesting detail to the outside of the home. However, the fluid, semicircular curve can also present a window decorating quandary. If the bow window features separate windows beneath curved molding, there may be enough space to mount separate window shades on each. To mount one continuous valance over all of the windows, consider ordering a custom-made curved rod or mounting decorative panels at the sides of the bow to help frame the window in an inviting manner.

▲ THE LINE OF THE CURVED MOLDING over this bow window is outlined with a metal rod, custom fitted to hold the pleated valance in place. Matching end panels border the window while individual woven-wood shades add textural quality and provide privacy when needed.

◄ CLEVER DRAPERY RINGS with threaded ends were secured into the wood molding above the bow window, eliminating the need for a curved rod. Mounting panels within the bow hides the sides of the woven shades, which are mounted at angles above the windows.

BEYOND SQUARE WINDOWS

Windows have undergone a creative revolution and are now available in a wide variety of shapes, including round, oval, octagonal, hexagonal, and triangular. Of course when it comes to treating these specialties, you'll need to come up with some creative solutions that work with the contours. Sometimes they're actually best left alone, but if treated, any window décor added should serve as a secondary point of interest. When a functional window covering is needed for privacy, custom-made wood shutters cut to fit the shape of the window may provide the solution, or a simple wood cornice trimmed with molding can cap the window, hiding a cellular shade from view.

▲ A BEAUTIFULLY SHAPED octagonal window adds cottage appeal in this loft-style bedroom. To close off the window at night, the homeowner had a hinged shutter custom crafted to fit the shape, and the wood was stained to complement the exposed beams and headboard.

◀ CREATIVELY ENGINEERED stationary panels form virtual columns along the sides of these cathedral-style windows. Wood cornices, stained in a rich tone to provide added drama, are mounted at the side of the trapezoid windows, drawing the eye up to the striking shapes above.

STYLES FOR DOORS

While the style of the treatment chosen for a door does not have to match the designs on the windows, there needs to be a feeling of continuity among all units. Using the same fabric is the easiest way to form a harmonious bond between windows and doors. You can also treat a door with a hard window treatment such as a new sliding *shoji* (pronounced "show-gee") screen while choosing fabric for the windows. Valances and shades are particularly suited to doors but keep in mind factors like clearances needed for swinging French doors and head room when walking through a door opening. You'll want to mount valances high above the door, but be sure to mount all other treatments in the room at the same height if possible. Roman shades mounted directly on the door above the glass are a clever solution as well.

Tips for Selecting Door Décor

- Determine the clearance a door needs when it swings. You shouldn't have to duck under a treatment when entering or exiting.

- Mount treatments at ceiling height to lengthen the look of the door.

- The material a door is made of should be considered when mounting directly on the door. Metal doors will require special drill bits and screws for installation.

- Consider a dual treatment—stationary panels for a decorative effect and shades for privacy.

▶ INSTALLING THE DRAPES at ceiling height creates a dramatic entrance to this office. Light from the transom windows above the doors can be regulated with the woven-wood shade mounted beneath the panels. The angular lines of the room are accentuated by the color-blocked fabric.

Treating Doors

Doors require special attention when it comes to selecting a treatment style. The design needs to add decorative dimension to the room, blend in with other window treatments, and provide privacy when needed.

▲ SINCE THERE WAS PLENTY of space surrounding the doors, the homeowner was able to stack drapery panels on the walls, enabling the doors to swing freely. Centering the drapery pole in the wall space between the door and ceiling spotlights the decorative metal pole.

▲ INDIVIDUAL SHADES fashioned in the same fabric used on the windows within this room are mounted directly on French doors, uniting the doors and windows. The shades pull up to a minimal depth when not in use or can be left at half-mast to highlight the print in the fabric.

▲ THE SIMPLE, CLEAN LINES of a *shoji* screen add visual interest to this bedroom while preserving floor space. The lightweight, translucent panels slide along an aluminum top track that is hidden from view by wood molding.

Functions of Window Treatments

WINDOW TREATMENTS CAN PROVIDE more than just good looks. A well-designed window dressing helps establish the mood of a room, whether the overall feel is glamorous or casual. Fabrics help create personality by adding color, texture, and dimension while reinforcing the color theme of the furnishings and accessories. Some window treatments also can provide privacy, such as long drapery panels that traverse along a pole or a stylish fabric shade that can be let down in the evening. Light control is also a benefit of panels and shades, especially when room-darkening linings are added.

To conserve energy, treatments can be backed with insulated linings that trap out the summer heat and winter cold. Noise is also a problem that can be remedied by layering insulated draperies over window shades to reduce sounds from the outdoors.

▼ A SET OF FRENCH DOORS along a wall is showcased with flowing panels tied onto rings, enabling the drapes to close quickly for privacy. The same fabric was used on the window in the seating alcove, but a Roman shade was better suited for the small window.

What Does Your Room Need?

To determine the best window treatment style to meet the needs in the room, ask yourself the following questions.

- **DECORATIVE APPEAL:** Is the treatment just for ornamental impact?

- **FABRIC SELECTION:** Are the treatments meant to be statements or accents?

- **WARMING TOUCH:** Does the room feel austere and need to be visually warmed?

- **PRIVACY AND LIGHT CONTROL:** Do you want the treatment to open and close?

- **ENERGY-SAVING PROPERTIES:** Should the treatment reduce energy consumption?

- **NOISE CONTROL:** Do you need to block outdoor sounds?

- **ILLUSION EFFECTS:** Do you want to hide room flaws or visually alter the window size?

▲ IN THIS SKYLINE APARTMENT, picture windows are bordered with a simple valance that pulls up at the sides, allowing a dramatic sweep of fabric to showcase the breathtaking view. The treatment is purely decorative, while blinds hidden beneath the valance provide privacy when called for.

◄ PRIVACY WAS THE MAIN CONCERN in this bedroom, which features triple windows and transom doors. To work with the monochromatic decorating theme, white Roman shades were mounted over each window, directly on the doors, and on the transoms above the doors, providing light control and privacy while adding simplistic appeal.

THE MASKING EFFECT

You can use window décor creatively to hide unattractive structural elements in a room. Covering an unsightly wall with sumptuous panels or disguising windows without trimwork by surrounding the glass in a lovely fabric are cost-efficient ways to beautify a setting without remodeling. Sheer panels continue to be the easiest way to hide less-than-perfect windows or to block an unsightly view. Handsome wood shutters can be used to encase tired windows, bringing new vitality to the setting. Create an illusion by placing window treatments at ceiling height or to the side, making a small window look substantial, or visually lengthen short windows with floor-length side panels.

▲ A SHORT, SQUAT WINDOW in a nursery was quickly enlarged by placing a shade high above it. To carry the height illusion throughout the room, drapery panels were mounted at the same point above the door.

▼ THE TALL WINDOWS flanking the sides of the fireplace appeared narrow and out of proportion with the grand scale of this room. To provide the illusion of added width and height sheer white panels swagged over drapery rods were cut 1 ft. wider than the windows, allowing the fabric to flow down the wall.

◄ THE BEAUTIFUL ANGULAR LINES of this ceiling are accentuated with a bamboo rod placed below an angled peak. When pulled closed, the black background fabric draws the eye up to the circular window above.

CHALLENGE: Small Windows

The windows on opposite sides of the fireplace are short and narrow in proportion to the scale of the wall and formality of the living area. The homeowner didn't want window treatments to draw attention to the small appearance of the windows.

SOLUTION: Floor-length panels were mounted just below the ceiling's edge to draw focus away from the windows and up to the spectacular tray ceiling. Stacking the panels onto the wall space at the sides of the window continues the illusion, making the window appear larger than it is. Sheer Roman shades further disguise the windows, allowing diffused light into the room while providing a softening effect.

► WINDOW TREATMENTS CAN CREATE optical illusions within a room. Small windows appear taller and wider in scale with the addition of floor-to-ceiling panels. The wheat-colored damask used here makes a soothing statement in a room filled with neutral tones.

FABRIC AND COLOR CHOICES

Choosing fabric is fun. While you don't need to be a professional decorator to select the right fabric for your windows, you should take the following ideas into consideration. The durability of the fabric is key in making sure the finished treatment will hold up over time. Cotton is the most commonly used and most versatile natural fiber. Cotton fabrics include sateen, damask, velvet, twill, chintz, sail cloth, and mattelasse. Linen is another all-purpose, natural fiber featuring a distinguished texture that looks great in informal valance, shade and panel styles.

Noted for its lustrous sheen and brilliant array of colors, silk is the most popular choice for luxurious window decorating. Due to the delicate nature of the fiber, silk must always be lined and interlined to prevent sun and moisture damage. A less-expensive, more-durable substitute for silk is polyester. A faux-silk polyester has the look of the real thing with the benefit of synthetic, man-made fibers that are long lasting and will remain colorfast, even with extended sun exposure. Other suitable acrylic choices include tapestries that are often polycotton blends, brocade, chenille, and moiré.

▲ DECIDING ON A FABRIC depends on the look you wish to create. Stunning silks and faux-silk polyesters add traditional elegance to a room, and many feature eye-catching embroidery designs, brilliant plaids and stripes, or interesting solid colors.

The Impact of Color

Different colors evoke emotional responses, making you feel a certain way when you spend time in the room. Here are some of the feelings that are elicited from color.

- BLACK—dramatic, sophisticated
- BLUE—peaceful, serene
- BROWN—nurtured, secure
- GREEN—refreshed, comforted
- ORANGE—radiant, creative
- PINK— lighthearted, youthful
- PURPLE—passionate, spiritual
- RED—stimulated, excited
- YELLOW—energetic, optimistic
- WHITE—pure, calm

▲ THE SURFACE OF VELVET provides subtle textural effects when the light shines in. Velvets feature a napped texture, so the color changes when viewed from different directions. Positioning the fabric with the nap running down provides a more uniform appearance.

◀ SILK DRAPERIES have a radiant sheen that is noticeable from across a room. This drape was pleated at the top by folding along specific stripes, allowing the inside of each pleat to fan out and reveal brilliant red color. Lining and interlining silk drapes ensures long-lasting wear.

▼ THESE RED DAMASK draperies create a stimulating effect when contrasted with the clean and calming white walls. Black accessories serve as interesting accents, adding dramatic flair.

Fabric Selection

THE PROCESS OF CHOOSING FABRIC can be overwhelming. This is understandable since there are thousands of decorator fabrics from which to choose. We've all heard not to grocery shop on an empty stomach. Keep that thought in mind before shopping for fabrics. Make sure your idea folder is full and well thought out before you set out the door. Decide if you want the windows to be major attractions within the room or if you want them to fade into the setting, letting other decorative highlights take the spotlight. This will help you narrow down the background color choice for the fabric. Bold colors pop, drawing attention; soft colors recede. Look at your existing furnishings and develop an idea about what type of fabric would look best—a solid, small print, stripe, or large-scale print. Remember to keep prints in scale with the setting—for instance, a small floral would look out of place on a soaring window.

▲ WHEN A VIBRANT PRINT IS USED, the window treatment becomes a vivid focal point. Since the background color of the valance and the wall are similar hues, the treatment recesses into the wall even though the print is dominant.

◄ THESE MINIMALIST SWAGS provide just the right touch above a row of leaded glass windows. The playful mini-plaid ruffle accentuating the gentle curve of the swags provides balanced contrast to the vibrant green fabric. Mounting the swags inside each window showcases the elegant molding.

▲ LIGHT-FILLED TRANSOM WINDOWS and the sweeping view in a dining area are not compromised when decorative panels are mounted at the edge of all windows. Accents of black throughout the space—the subtle black stripes in the fabric, iron drapery rods, chandelier, and dining chairs—provide contrast yet allow the setting to take center stage.

HOW MUCH TO SPEND?

Window treatments are an investment, but you can easily mix and match options so that you spend the most money on windows in high-visibility rooms, like the kitchen and family room, and less on those in private spaces, like bedrooms and bathrooms. Whether you plan to buy off-the-shelf window treatments, sew your own, or hire a decorator, shop around, as prices vary from source to source. Using the Internet is a great way to discover a world of resources.

▲ A PROFESSIONAL DESIGN CONSULTANT offered advice for the style of this entire room, then the owner followed the plan by painting and ordering the window treatments online for quick results.

▲ IF YOU'RE DECISION-SHY when it comes to decorating, hiring a design consultant will boost your confidence and help you make choices that reflect your personality and lifestyle.

Hiring a Decorator

Turning to an interior decorator for help with custom window treatment design may turn out to be a smart investment. Today's decorators are more like design consultants, offering knowledge and support as you work through the decision-making process together. Referrals are a good way to find skilled decorators, but interview the person to be sure you can work together. A good decorator will respond to your opinions, but remember, you've hired this person for their design expertise. When she offers knowledge, listen. Be up front about how much you wish to spend, and find out if she charges by the hour. You may find that several hours are all you need to get a plan together that you can initiate on your own.

Price Comparisons

There are many ways to obtain window treatments. Shopping around will reveal the best option for you. For custom treatments, get price quotes from several sources. Sewing your own treatments is always a money-saver, but you must invest precious time. There are several companies that offer quality custom treatments online. Before you buy the fabric be sure to order swatches so that you can see and feel the fabrics first. While an interior designer may seem costly, you are paying for unique fabrics and trims that are not available to the general public. Here are relative costs from one option to another.

	Basic Roman Shade	Swag and Jabot	Drapery Panels
Ready-mades	$	$	$
Sewing your own	$	$ to $$	$$
Custom—Decorating store	$$ to $$$	$$$	$$ to $$$
Custom—Online	$$	$$	$$
Custom—Hiring decorator	$$$	$$$$	$$$ to $$$$

$ low $$ moderate $$$ pricey $$$$ high

For custom options, price comparisons include fabric and labor only; decorative trims, installation, and rod for drapery panels are extra.

▲ CUSTOM-MADE SWAG AND JABOT window treatments can be expensively styled in luxurious fabrics and trims or created in less costly combinations.

◄ BEFORE YOU REPLACE older window treatments with what could become a costly solution, try reworking what you already have. By simply adding pinch pleats, these drapery panels got an extended life, and the room benefited from an updated look.

▲ ROMAN SHADES OFFER VALUE because they beautify the window and function as privacy barriers. Prices will vary greatly depending upon the style. Flat shades are the least expensive, while hobbled shades with cascading folds that remain intact when the shade is lowered are pricier.

Privacy and Light Control

Nεw innovations in the world of shutters, shades, and blinds are making our houses easier to live in. Technology has helped us come a long way—it's now possible to click a remote and lower all the window coverings in a room. Research has spawned the development of window products that are making our homes safer, too. Worried about UV rays damaging your furnishings? Invisible window film can be applied to the glass to block harmful sunlight. Concerned about the safety of children around shade cords? New continuous-loop cord tracks and cordless shades are completely child-proof. Even if you're just looking to cut sun glare during certain times of the day, semitransparent solar blinds can be installed to control light yet still allow you to see outdoors.

As you dress your windows, think of it as a layering process where the first treatments to consider are those closest to the window. Cellular shades, woven-wood blinds, custom shutters, or *shoji* screens are just a few of the choices that add privacy to rooms while helping to control the light. Many of these products can stand alone as window décor or can become part of a beautiful combination when topped with a decorative valance or matched with a set of stunning drapery panels.

◄ SHUTTERS ADD ARCHITECTURAL dimension to a window, especially when painted the same color as the trimwork. These traditional-style shutters fold back at the sides of the windows to reveal a breathtaking view, while allowing maximum light and ventilation into the room.

Shutters

SHUTTERS HAVE EXISTED FOR CENTURIES, dating back to ancient Greece when louvers, the moveable slats within the shutter, were made of marble. While materials may have changed, today's shutters still add beautiful, functional styling to windows. Wood shutters can be luxuriously rich in appearance, sporting highly polished finishes reflecting the unique character of the hardwood grains. A new crop of less costly alternates include faux-wood shutters, made from poly-satin compounds, ideal for bathrooms and sun porches where heat and humidity are factors. Plantation-style shutters now include louvers up to 4½ in. wide and can feature one-tilt operation, where all slats move when just one is touched. Rear-tilting systems eliminate the middle rail bar for unobstructed viewing through the louvers. Even old windows can be enhanced by installing custom shutter units that are framed in handsome molding, completely masking what lies behind.

▲ THESE PATIO DOORS are fitted with a custom shutter unit that is installed on a sliding track directly over the doors, allowing the panels to bypass as they glide. An added benefit is that the shutters don't intrude on the floor space.

▶ WHEN OPENED, these bedroom shutters fold back on the wall, giving the windows an expansive appearance. Tilting the louvers to reveal the taupe walls creates an interesting design effect, making the windows focal points in the room.

▲ NARROW WINDOWS bordering a fireplace are hard to treat, especially when the mantel almost touches the side moldings. Shutters installed inside the window frame provide both light control and decorative appeal, eliminating the need for window treatments.

Creating a Mock Transom

Shutters can be used to create interesting illusions within a room. Transform an ordinary window into a mock transom style by covering three-fourths of the window with shutters, exposing a top row of glass. This works best if the window has mullions dividing the upper portion into rectangles, helping to form the distinctive transom look. Use this effect in bathrooms or other areas where privacy and light control are key. Choose between bi-fold shutters that fold to the side during the day or a one-piece shutter with louvers that tilt to allow sunlight in, providing filtered, daytime privacy.

▶ SHORT SHUTTERS allow the top of a window to peek through, creating the look of a transom window. The addition of a creative swag treatment draws your eye up to the transom, while the side tails help show off the decorative tile work.

ARCH-TOP SOLUTIONS

▲ A PALLADIAN WINDOW is surrounded by a plantation shutter unit, crafted to create the look of a transom. The wide louvers allow for easier viewing and help bring the outdoors in. The eyebrow arch was left untouched to draw attention to the lofty ceiling.

▶ SHUTTERS SHAPED to fit an arch-top window look as beautiful closed as they do open. Combining this with clean shutter panels on the rest of the window unit keeps the attention on the specialty window.

Shutters in the Bathroom

Faux-wood shutters made from poly-satin compounds are guaranteed not to warp, fade, chip, or peel, making them an excellent choice for steamy bathrooms. Quality and price vary, so be sure to shop around.

▲ **SHUTTERS WERE MOUNTED** to highlight this transom arch and provide light-filtering privacy over an inviting spa. Decorative sheer window dressings, creatively installed on drapery tieback holders, soften the angular lines of the shutters.

▲ **THIS BAY WINDOW** above a whirlpool tub was subtly decorated with shutters for privacy and function. A mock transom look was created on the windows by installing shortened shutters, adding to the elegant appeal of the majestic center arch window.

▶ **PRIVACY, ALWAYS KEY** in bathrooms, was addressed here with shutters mounted café style on a side window yet covering the entire window above the tub. The wide louvers and mounting position allows the homeowner to enjoy the tranquil view while soaking in the bath.

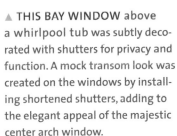

SPECIAL SHAPES

▲ CUSTOM SHUTTERS in this studio apartment were placed over triangular windows to solve the problem of street lights peeking through at night. An expandable wand helps to reach the louvers, making it simple to open and close them as needed.

▲ THESE HOMEOWNERS chose custom shutters to accentuate the interesting curved shape of a nursery window and to help darken the room for nap time. Choosing white for the shutter and trim color allows for versatility when it's time for a more grown-up room.

▶ WOOD SHUTTERS WITH a furniture-quality finish were custom made to encase the glass on these French doors, allowing room for the handles to move freely. Since the windows lacked trimwork, shutter units with elegant moldings were installed over the openings, giving the room a whole new appearance.

Ordering Custom Shutters

Shutters can be custom ordered in an array of stained, painted, glazed, or crackle finishes. Many manufacturers offer scores of stain colors, and some have custom services where they can match a sample of an existing paint or stain color used in the room. Specialty windows in all shapes and sizes can be custom fitted with shutters; however, be sure to have a professional come out to measure and install them for you. Shop for customized products through a local decorator or search the Internet to reveal reputable dealers in your area. Shutters are an investment in your home and it pays to find a company that stands behind its work, offering guarantees on the final product.

▲ STUNNING LEADED GLASS adorns the top of these combination shutters, adding architectural splendor to a corner setting. The mix of glass and wood transforms run-of-the-mill windows into striking assets.

◄ THIS BATHROOM'S country interior was enhanced by painting traditional-style shutters to match the charming wainscoting. With the tub so close to the windows, shutters provide the needed privacy while creating a unified look on the corner-style windows.

Woven-Wood Shades

WOVEN-WOOD SHADES, a contemporary version of 1960s-style bamboo blinds, are one the most popular window coverings today. Woven shades are making headlines for a number of reasons, the foremost being the "green" factor: The shades are made from natural reeds, grasses, and woods that provide rich coloring and textural details. Found in many styles from roll-up to classic fold-up designs, they are manufactured by hand or machine. Woven woods can be found in light translucent forms when made from delicate reeds and grasses. When rattan, bamboo, and other wood shafts are woven together, the colors are bolder and more light can be blocked; for true darkness, a blackout lining can be added. A matching valance can add a finishing touch along the top edge while hiding the lifting mechanisms you may glimpse through a loosely woven shade.

▲ THE NATURAL BEAUTY of woven-wood shades is accentuated here by the gracious curve of brilliant white window moldings. Shades come in any shape, and the variations in color and texture add defining interest to this dining area.

► THESE WINDOWS are cohesively joined with individual woven grass shades mounted within the window frames. A reed coffee table along with the bamboo rod that holds the stationary panels in place offer complementary touches in the room.

How Wide Can a Shade Be?

Woven-wood shades up to 120 in. wide can be made to work comfortably. Wider shades work best when made from lightweight grasses since you will be pulling the bulk up and down each time you operate the shade. One wide, expansive shade provides a cohesive, neat look across multiple windows. However, if you're concerned about the weight of one large shade, placing several across a wide window is another option. If there is enough room for mounting within the window frame, individual shades can be installed there as well. Or, two or three shades can be installed side by side on the same head rail, with a matching valance positioned across all. For shades over 72 in. wide, use a continuous-loop lifting system that provides a child-safe cord attached to the window frame.

▼ A TOP-DOWN, bottom-up option is shown here (see the sidebar on p. 135), allowing the shades to be positioned café style across the windows. One extra wide shade graces a set of windows to keep with the simplistic, contemporary feel of the room.

▶ MATCHSTICK-STYLE SHADES made from sand-colored reeds add a semitransparent layer to this trio of windows. The loose weave allows the sun to gently diffuse through the shades, drawing attention to their delicate and unique texture.

▼ REEDS AND GRASSES are popular choices for woven shades since the weaves are more delicate in appearance, allowing light to filter through tiny spaces and breaks. Some materials are water stained for interesting color enhancements while others are left in their natural form.

▶ THE CREAM COLOR scheme in this kitchen is tastefully interrupted with textural woven shades mounted above all windows. The natural coloring of the shades brings warmth to the kitchen, eliminating the need for fabric treatments.

Enhancing Woven Woods

Customizing woven shades is a fun way to add color and texture to windows. Decorative braids, fabric bands, a fabric topper, and even drapery tiebacks are just a few ways to spark interest.

▶ **WITHOUT THE SIMPLE** fabric valances, these roll-up blinds would have made less of a visual impression. The neutral print in the fabric brings out the natural highlights in the woven reeds, providing a unified look to the windows.

▶ **TASSEL TIEBACKS,** normally found at the side of the window, can be used more creatively when featured down the front of a roll-up matchstick shade. This shade is bordered with a subtle damask fabric, and the tiebacks were simply attached to the shade front.

▲ **FABRIC BRAIDS AND EDGE BANDINGS** can be ordered in a wide array of colors, prints, and widths, turning an ordinary shade into one custom matched to a room's décor. While such details will cost more, the overall effect is well worth the price.

CHALLENGE: Woven Woods in a Bay

This homeowner wanted to place woven-wood shades in her bay window for texture and to manage the sunlight, but she wasn't sure what size shades would best suit the windows.

SOLUTION: The first step is to determine if the shades can be mounted inside the window frames or if they must be placed on the outside of the window.

INSIDE MOUNTS: For windows featuring handsome moldings, inside mounts are desirable; however, there must be enough space within the frame to accommodate the head rail of the shade. Some woven shades require up to 4 in. of unobstructed depth, and you also must consider any window handles or locks that may interfere when the shade is lowered.

OUTSIDE MOUNTS: In this case, the shade is mounted on the window molding or wall. If there is wall space between the windows, you can highlight each individual window by having the shades cut the same width as the outside molding measurement. Or, to make the windows appear wider and to create a more continuous look, mount shades cut wider than the window with their sides almost touching in the angled corners of the bay.

▲ THIS SUNNY BAY WINDOW in a child's room was accentuated with woven-wood shades mounted inside the frame of each window, allowing the shades to be encased by the brilliant white molding. The natural beauty of the woven rattan coordinates well with the pine furnishings in the room.

◄ THESE WOVEN-WOOD SHADES were mounted outside the window molding within this bay setting, allowing the shades to stand alone as individual decorative focal points. The pale blue walls provide powerful contrast to the textural surface of the shades.

Mounting Woven Shades on Transom Windows

The weave and texture of the materials used in woven woods allows the shades to filter rather than block light. This characteristic provides the perfect solution for use on transom windows, as the transom can be covered yet still remain visible beneath the translucent shade. Look for loosely woven shades in lighter colors constructed from thin reeds or grasses that will have the most show-through when the shade is lowered. Woven woods also can be pulled up to stack tightly above a transom when you want to display the full effect of the window.

▼ A LAYERED EFFECT can be achieved with a woven shade and side panels mounted over a transom, allowing light to filter through the shade while still revealing the elegance of the window. The shade also can be pulled up to a minimal stacking depth to bring full focus to the transom.

▲ THE STUNNING WINDOW in a sun-filled kitchen resulted in sun glare at certain times of the day. A natural colored woven-wood shade was chosen for the light-filtering effect; the shade not only reduces glare but silhouettes the window beneath when the sun shines through.

Lined Woven Shades

Since woven shades only filter light, you must add lining to block the sun from penetrating entirely. The best option is to order shades with lining stitched directly to the back, allowing the lining to fold along with the shade. Lining also can hang separately behind the shade, though you will have to raise and lower the two layers separately. For maximum room darkness, be sure to select a total blackout lining. Other linings will act more as light filters, providing only partial blockage. White or off white drapery linings are commonly used and most provide moisture resistance.

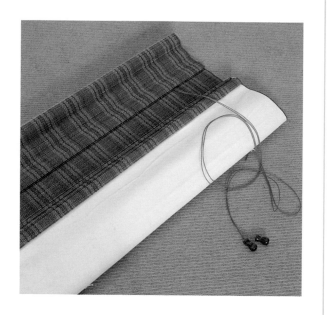

► **ADDING A LINING** to a woven-wood shade is a must if you want to darken a room. This lining was stitched directly to the shade back and encased in the hem so it will fold along with the shade during operation.

► TOP-DOWN, BOTTOM-UP SHADES can be motorized to operate from a hard-wired wall switch or remote control. All of these shades can be raised to cover half the window or pulled to the top for total privacy. Motorizing the shades offers timesaving convenience in rooms with multiple windows.

Motorizing Shades

One of the biggest developments in the shade and blind industry is the use of motorization. With the click of a remote or flick of a wall switch you can lift, tilt, and lower all of the shades in one room or in an entire house. Woven-wood shades, as well as cellular and pleated shades, roller shades, micro blinds, and wood or sheer horizontal blinds up to 2 in. wide, can be motorized. It's a great option for oversized shades and blinds that are heavy to operate by hand.

Types of Motorization

There are three basic types of motorization for window coverings:

HARD-WIRED: Hard-wiring allows a wall switch to be installed that can control a room or the entire house by remote control. Hire an electrician to run 120 VAC wires in your walls, conforming to local codes. While the best time to install wiring is when walls are open, such as when you're building a new home or adding an addition, existing shades also can be hard-wired.

BATTERY: Existing shades and blinds can be retrofitted with a battery-operated motor that slides into the head rail of the shade. When not in operation, a sleeper mode ensures a five- to ten-year life for lithium batteries. A decorator or authorized dealer will retrofit your existing coverings or may offer do-it-yourself motor kits.

PLUG IN: A plug-in style motor is fitted to an existing shade or blind with a cord that plugs into an outlet. This option is only suitable if the cord can be hidden beneath long drapery panels.

Benefits of Motorization

- Raises, lowers, and tilts shades and blinds at the touch of a button or switch
- Prolongs life of products because there is no manual pulling or tugging
- Eliminates cord tangling for child and pet safety
- Wireless wall timers can be installed to operate shades if you're away
- Ideal for large or hard to reach windows like skylights
- Automatic sun sensor options monitor sun intensity, operating shades accordingly

▲ **REMOTES FOR MOTORIZED** shades can employ infrared frequency, where you simply point the remote at the window, or be radio controlled, where you don't need a direct line of sight to operate the shades. Remotes can be programmed to operate windows separately or as a group within a room.

MOTORIZED WINDOW TREATMENT COMPONENTS

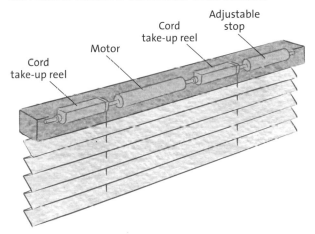

Cord take-up reel · Motor · Cord take-up reel · Adjustable stop

INSERTING A MOTOR INTO AN EXISTING ROLLER SHADE

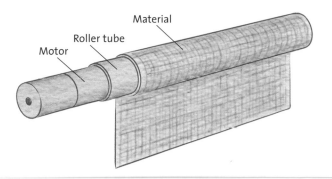

Material · Roller tube · Motor

Shades, Blinds, and Panel Tracks

NEW SHADES AND REFINEMENTS to longtime favorites offer decorative style, sun protection, and privacy for today's varied window styles. Pleated and cellular shades, available in a wide palette of colors, can be crafted to fit almost any window shape. Combination shades provide a new twist, layering pleated shades in stunning prints over solid roller shades. Solar shades eliminate sun glare on television and computer screens and offer UV sun protection yet still allow you to see the view outdoors. When no window treatment is preferred, invisible window films can be applied directly to the glass, filtering out heat and glare. To personalize wood or faux wood blinds, try banding them with a striking decorative tape. For a more unique touch, use a panel track or *shoji* screen instead of vertical blinds; the sliding screens can feature rice paper or interesting fabrics.

▲ WOOD BLINDS OFFER timeless beauty and are available in a rich variety of stain and paint finishes. The tilting slats come in 1-in. to 3-in. widths; the larger the width the better the viewing capability. Adding a decorative tape can transform blinds into stand-alone fashion statements.

▼ COMBINATION SHADES are two styles that operate independently but are mounted on one head rail for easy installation. Here, flat fabric panels were mounted on shortened rods on both sides of the window to add style to the walls and provide a framing effect around the shades.

▲ CELLULAR SHADES are available in cordless designs that retract with a simple touch, providing added safety if you have small children or pets. The shades compress to a minimal depth when raised to the highest position and will fade from view if color-matched to the walls.

CHALLENGE: Expansive Bedroom Window

A transom topped window in this contemporary bedroom posed privacy concerns for the homeowners. They were looking for a functional window covering that would maintain the open feel of the room while adding style to the setting.

SOLUTION: A panel track system was installed across the window. The panels glide open during the day and rest along the wall, fully exposing the glass. When the panels are closed, laminated rice paper allows light to filter through while providing a privacy barrier. The grid work on the screen complements the mullions in the transom above and provides an aesthetic element in the room. A light birch frame was chosen here; many other woods and finishes are available.

▼ **SHOJI SCREENS** with lightly stained frames were selected to accent the wood tones of the existing furniture. The screens glide easily and do not take up floor space as drapery panels would. The clean styling of these screens makes them an excellent choice for minimalist settings.

SHADES

▶ **TWO-IN-ONE SHADES** provide multiple options for style and light control. You can position a pleated shade, like this one made from a white burnout sheer, at any height. The solar shade mounted underneath has equal flexibility and will block the sun while darkening the room.

▲ **THERE ARE MANY INTERESTING** color and fabric choices available for combination shades. Darker colors provide more room-darkening ability and add more visual impact when a translucent sheer is placed on top.

▲ **TO PRESERVE THE VIEW** in this seaside kitchen, cellular shades were mounted inside the frames across a row of transom-style windows. The shades offer the flexibility the vacationing cooks need—ease of use, minimal stacking depth, and sunlight control during the afternoon.

◄ PLEATED AND CELLULAR SHADES are now available in a range of fabrics that include subtle prints, jacquard weaves, geometric shapes, and textural effects that can create impact in a decorating scheme.

Solar Shades

Solar shades, made from specially designed woven mesh fabrics, cut down on excessive sun glare while offering fade protection to fabric window coverings, furniture, and rugs. The shades are often sold as roller blinds that zip up to wrap around a roller, or they can be made in a fold-up roman style. The fabric weave allows diffused light through while filtering out harmful UV rays. For greater sun-blocking ability, select a tightly woven mesh fabric in a light color. Darker meshes and open weaves will allow more sunlight through. Since all solar shades are semitransparent during the day and night, traversing panels can be added for privacy.

▲ MESH SOLAR SHADES were installed in this family room that has a tendency to become excessively hot as the day progresses. The black shades provide soothing protection from sun glare yet still allow the homeowner to check on children playing outside.

◄ ROLLER-STYLE SOLAR shades can be whisked up and out of sight, providing function beneath flowing drapery panels in this dining room. Since the shades are translucent, panels were added to provide privacy when needed and to add style to the windows.

BLINDS

▶ MOUNTING SEPARATE SHADES instead of one large one draws attention to each individual window. It also allows individual shades to be drawn for privacy or light blocking.

▼ THE NATURAL BEAUTY of wood blinds is enhanced when light peaks through the slats, giving a rich appearance to this alcove of windows. Before the blinds were installed, viewing the television during the day was difficult.

▲ SINCE THIS ARCH-TOP bedroom window had no surrounding molding, the shade was cut several inches wider than the opening so the slats would extend onto the wall. This complements the contemporary feel of the room.

Where to Shop for Blinds and Shades

Price, durability, and convenience are three factors to consider when deciding where to shop for blinds and shades. If you have a number of rooms to decorate start by spending less for window coverings in secondary rooms and more for those in hub rooms. Remember, window coverings are an asset to your home and may pay for themselves when your home is sold.

HOME CENTERS: This is the lowest cost option where you will find a limited selection of ready-to-buy items that can be cut to size. Many of the shades and blinds offered are made of composite woods or plastic, allowing you to achieve the look you want on a reasonable budget. You also can order a limited selection of custom products.

CATALOGS AND INTERNET: If you don't mind installing shades yourself, catalogs and Internet sites offer great selections along with plenty of advice and instructions. Be sure to order samples of the materials first so you can view the fabric in your room. Prices vary greatly but are often low to moderate.

DEALER OR DECORATOR: If you have many windows, a dealer or decorator could be your best option. He can offer the best selection of products and may come up with a fresh idea for you to consider. A professional will handle the measuring and installation and if a problem arises, you can rely on him for help.

◄ DECORATIVE FABRIC TAPES add vertical design lines to wood blinds and can be used to accent other colors within the room. Here, the dark tones of the wood and furnishings in this room are reflected in the chocolate brown tapers on the blinds.

PANEL-TRACK SYSTEMS

▲ SHEER FABRIC PANELS were installed along a wall of windows, bringing texture to this sleek bedroom. The top of each panel is attached to a sliding track with hook-and-loop tape, allowing for easy removal when cleaning. Weighted bars in the bottom hems keep the fabric taut.

CHALLENGE: Sun Glare in a Family Room

Walls of glass in this poolside family room created a greenhouse effect during afternoon hours—the room became increasingly warm and too uncomfortable to enjoy. In addition, harsh sunlight streaming through the arch-top window made television viewing impossible at times.

SOLUTION: Specially developed window film was professionally installed directly on the interior glass, blocking UV rays and eliminating sun glare. The films are available in different grades, and the homeowners chose one that rejects over 65 percent of total solar energy, a decision that dramatically reduced heat buildup and air conditioning costs. The films are scratch-resistant, a good option for people who have small children or pets. A manufacturer's warranty guarantees that the adhesive used to apply the film will hold up for years and that it will not discolor over time.

▲ WINDOW FILM ACTS like sunglasses by preventing sun glare and UV penetration while homeowners can still enjoy the view. A professional installs the film with a special adhesive, resulting in an invisible barrier on the window that will reduce energy costs.

◀ THESE HOMEOWNERS found that the reduction in energy costs helped defray the initial investment of window film. Film is priced by the square footage covered; prices vary depending upon labor and film type chosen.

Creative Window Toppers

One of the quickest ways to add eye-catching pizzazz to a room is by adding a cleverly designed window topper. "Topper" is a broad term used to describe any fabric window covering that creates interest at the top of a window. Commonly referred to as valances, toppers can add instant impact to the overall design of a room in subtle or dramatic ways. In addition to adding visual appeal, toppers also can hide a privacy shade or a curtain rod. Arch-top and transom windows, which can be challenging to decorate, are perfectly suited to toppers since these window treatment styles can enhance such stunning architectural details. The right combination of topper style and fabric choice can transform an ordinary-looking room into one you'll enjoy spending time in.

◄ TOP TREATMENTS DRAW the eye upward and can create a stunning focal point on a window. A pleated valance is a great way to showcase an interesting motif in a fabric like the medallion print shown here. The front pleats add dimension while the side kick pleats add flirty style.

Pleated Styles

PLEATED VALANCES COME IN many shapes and sizes, but all have two elements in common: the pleats are formed at the top edge of the treatment, and the fabric lays flat between the pleat folds. The pleated valance is the most versatile of all valance types, so much so that you could pick variations of this one style and decorate windows in every room in your home, without any two looking exactly alike.

Pleats add dimension and often help to highlight a decorative print or texture in a fabric. But it's important to select fabric of proper weight for a pleated valance: light to mid-weight fabrics work best because they pleat well without adding bulk at the top edge. Be sure to line all valances to prevent show-through of the print when the sun is shining through the treatment.

▼ VIBRANT FABRICS are best suited to window treatment styles with simple lines. The bold red-and-white plaid of this pleated valance takes center stage while its straight shape suits the pattern.

▲ PLEATED BALLOON VALANCES offer tailored looks that are softened by the fullness at the bottom edge. The prominent stripe centered on each scallop adds a bold splash of red against the butter-colored walls. Piping across the valance adds a designer touch.

5 Reasons for Selecting a Pleated Valance

- Offers a tailored, sophisticated look
- Looks great in rooms of any style
- Economizes on fabric because minimal yardage is required
- Highlights decorative details such as fringe or bead trim
- Creates a statement with vibrant prints or textured fabrics

CREATIVE SOLUTION

CHALLENGE: Arch-Top Triple Window

When the view outside is the focal point, the window treatment style needs to enhance—not distract from—the setting.

SOLUTION: The elegant shape of this pleated valance gently sweeps across the center window, with pleats cleverly positioned to continue the vertical lines of the arch top above. The valance dips lower over the side windows, adding depth without competing for your eye's attention. The ends of the window are framed with softly folded jabots that cascade outward. Even though the fabric features a large-scale print, the white background lends a light and airy feel and helps the treatment fade into the woodwork. The decorative trim along the edge of the valance forms a dividing line between the window and the view outside.

▲ THIS CUSTOM ROOM CALLS for a creatively designed window treatment that will reflect the graceful curve of the beamed ceiling in addition to highlighting the arch of the triple window.

▲ THE SPACING BETWEEN THE PLEATS in this box-style valance is in perfect proportion with the windows below them.
The side windows each have one expanse of fabric between the pleats, while the center window features three sections.

Pleated Valances

The basic box-pleat valance can make a strong visual statement or add a subtle touch to a room's surroundings depending upon fabric choice.

▲ IF THE VALANCE and side panels were in a plain fabric, this window would simply fade into the blue walls. The colorful geometric check, however, brings the window to life. The valance and stationary side panels create a visual frame around the Roman shade.

▲ IF YOUR FABRIC has different motifs as part of the design, pick a couple to be highlighted across the valance. Here, several different print motifs are centered within each section of the valance, avoiding a repetitive look.

▶ LIKE OTHER PRINTS, plaids need to be carefully planned to highlight just the part of the fabric you want. Here, a delicate fringe trim accents the bottom edge with matching bias piping finishing off the top edge of the treatment. The valance was kept short to allow the transom windows to be seen.

▲ TO COMPLEMENT THE SIMPLICITY of this gorgeous kitchen setting, a neutral taupe-and-white check fabric was selected. The width of each scallop in the valance mimics the window pane width, and the shortened length allows the breathtaking view to be the focal point.

► UPDATING A PICTURE WINDOW with a romantic, pleated-festoon valance made out of silk creates a feel of casual elegance. The large scale of each festoon corresponds with the width of the window. Faux-crystal trim catches the sunlight and adds a luxurious touch.

What Size Pleats Are Right?

Whether you're making a basic box-pleat valance or a pleated balloon shade, the spacing between pleats is best determined by the size of the window. If your room features several "single" windows between 34 in. and 44 in. wide, (the range of standard-size windows), spacing the pleats 10 in. to 15 in. apart makes for pleasing proportions.

For rooms with larger double or triple windows, plan for 18 in. to 30 in. of space between the pleats to keep the treatments in scale with the window. As a general rule, keep the pleat spacing about the same for all of the window treatments in a room to ensure a unified look.

40-in. window with
10-in. pleat spacing

60-in. window with 20-in.
pleat spacing

▲ THESE WIDE CENTER SCALLOPS offer a fashionable look and are neatly sandwiched between the smaller cascading sides. The coordinating covered buttons and elegant tassel add stylish details.

▲ PLAN FOR SMALLER-WIDTH balloons across a double window for a fuller look. Here, the subtle plaid print is placed randomly on each balloon for an informal look. Mounting the treatment at ceiling height elongates the look of the window, a technique that helps balance the overall appearance.

New Look Cornices

ANY OF US REMEMBER the wood cornice from long ago—a heavily upholstered board with geometric shaping along the bottom edge. Cornices are making strong design statements again, updated to reflect the beauty of the new generation of windows in today's homes.

Cornices are often referred to as hard or soft window treatments. Hard cornices are made from wood or a wood-like material, and can stand alone when stained or painted, adding architectural detail to a window. Padded cornices (boards covered with quilt batting and then fabric) often feature shapes sculpted into the bottom edge. Soft cornices are made from fabric only, and their simple lines make them a perfect window treatment when styled in a beautiful print fabric. Both padded and soft cornices showcase fabric boldly, so it is important to choose a fabric that makes the kind of statement you're looking for in your room.

▲ SOFT CORNICES are cleverly cinched together along the top edges, forming handkerchief shapes that bring depth and dimension to the treatments. The lively floral print adds zest while the decorative fringe and cording provide finishing details that tie in with this eating area's decor.

▼ A THREE-TIERED SOFT CORNICE wraps around two walls of windows, creating a cohesive look between the different size windows while also hiding the drapery rods. The evenly spaced folds add dimension and interest to the rectangular cut of the treatment.

▲ SIMPLE STYLING is most effective when the right fabric and trim is selected. The unusual length of these soft cornices are enhanced by a delicate shape cut into their lower edge. Side panels in matching fabric anchor the cornices and provide a harmonious feel to the room.

▲ A SENSATIONAL WOOD CORNICE, hand-painted in muted stripes, creates a stunning accent for this seaside setting. The bottom edge, with its wave-like shape, mimics the movement of the ocean.

Positioning Prints for Maximum Impact

Soft cornice styles are the perfect treatment for prominent-print fabrics. When shopping for fabric, lay it out in the store as if you were creating the cornice so that you can visualize the way a flower or stripe will look in the finished treatment. Fold the fabric around a pleasing motif and step back to view it. If you choose to repeat the same motif in the flat expanses across the cornice, be sure that the print is not too overwhelming. Sometimes it's better to pick out two prints in a fabric and alternate their appearance across the cornice.

▶ A CRISP RED-AND-WHITE novelty scene sets a playful tone when showcased in the center of a simple, shaped cornice. The cording on the edges adds design emphasis.

▲ IN THIS NAUTICAL-THEMED ROOM, the ships appear to set sail across the horizon on the bow window's soft cornice. The consistency and movement of the pattern also encourages the eye up, making the room feel larger.

Soft Cornices

A soft cornice can fit inside the window frame for a delicate touch or outside to surround the window and house long panels or shades.

▲ A BOLD PRINT is the focal point in this kitchen eating area. Mounting the cornices inside the window frames not only showcases the molding, but also expands this bay window by dividing it into three individual windows.

◄ A LOFT WITH BRICK WALLS is transformed to a sophisticated level with a silk cornice and coordinating drapery panels. The intricate cut of the cornice's edge provides a delicate touch that contrasts with the broad expanse of the brick wall. The matching fabric shade helps to unify the look.

▲ THE MAJOR CHARACTERISTIC of all stagecoach-style cornices are layers of horizontal folds that give dimension to the treatment. Here, they bring visual appeal to both sides of the fireplace. The tapestry-weight fabric works beautifully, providing just the right balance next to the stonework.

▲ AN ELABORATELY CARVED wood cornice accented with crown molding not only serves as an architectural detail but also minimizes the wall of windows by housing drapery panels that can be closed for privacy.

▲ BE CREATIVE when looking for ways to embellish window treatments. Here, common antique nail heads were used to form a decorative trim, complementing the masculine setting.

▲ LEATHER CORNICES add a traditional touch in this home office, balancing the texture and dark colors of the furnishings. Even though the bay window extends higher than the door, the cornice is mounted at the same height as the door treatment, providing a continuous line around the room.

Combo Treatments

Draping a swag treatment over a straight cornice instantly transforms a plain window into a style worthy of showhouse status.

1. THE CORNICE: Start with a simple cornice as a backdrop for the swagged treatment. For existing wood cornices, you may choose to refinish the wood with a beautiful stain or paint it to match the wall color. To make a soft cornice backdrop, first decide how deep you want the cornice to be. Purchase decorator fabric, drapery lining, and a stiff interfacing to interline the treatment, which will help the treatment hold its shape. Stitch the three layers into a lined rectangle, adding decorative trim to the top and bottom edges if desired. Staple the treatment onto a 1-in. by 3-in. pine mounting board.

2. THE SWAGS: Purchase a commercial sewing pattern similar to the swag style shown here from your local fabric store. Make the individual swags, highlighting the bottom curved edges with decorative trim. Staple the swags to the top of the cornice board.

3. THE ROSETTES: Add rosettes from matching or contrasting fabric (for more on this see "Rosettes" on p. 174). Staple or pin the rosettes to the cornice where swags intersect.

▶ **THE SMALL-CHECK PRINT** on the soft cornice contrasts perfectly with the high-energy floral fabric found in the swags and drapery panel.

▲ **WITHOUT THE SWAG TREATMENT,** this wood cornice would look ordinary. The matching drapes mounted beneath the board help to pull the entire look together.

▲ A NO-FUSS CORNICE, softly padded in a mid-sized plaid fabric, is at home in this tailored sitting room. The drapes remain stationary with the tiebacks in place while the blinds are operational.

► THIS SOFT CORNICE wraps around the bow window to unify the six individual windows without obscuring the diner's view. The side panels are purely decorative, to frame the setting.

Wood Cornices

Many of the new looks in wood cornices include creatively designed shapes cut into the lower edges, highlighted with decorative painting, wallpaper cutouts, or unique fabrics. New materials used to make the cornices include thin plywood composites, which are pliable enough to bend around corners.

▼ ADD A TOUCH OF WHIMSY to a child's room by adhering pre-pasted wallpaper cutouts to a simple box cornice. The stars and moon theme can be carried through the room with galaxy-print bedding and accessories.

▲ THIS ORNATE CORNICE helps to unify this room's theme. It also serves as an anchor, since it can remain even if the home-owner chooses new bed linens.

► THE BOTTOM EDGE of this wallpapered cornice was cut to the shape of the decorative border to add extra definition. The drapery fabric was kept to a subtle stripe to highlight the intricate cornice.

Arch-Top Valances

ALMOST ALL newly constructed homes have arch windows. While beautiful to look at, arch windows can be difficult to treat because of their shape. Most designers choose to place window coverings below the arch to avoid the time-consuming task of making a curved window treatment. Some arches, however, call out for a window style to be mounted within the arched frame. Keeping the treatment design simple and understated is crucial so that the arch window remains the focus with the window covering serving as an accent.

▼ PROPORTION AND FABRIC SELECTION are the two most important elements at work here. The length of the balloon topper harmonizes with the long arch window as it covers just enough of the glass without becoming obtrusive. The neutral color of the fabric also helps the valance blend in with the setting so that the window remains the focal point.

▲ FABRIC PANELS MOUNTED on a bendable composite board are tied in poufs to simulate the clouds adorning this ceiling. Ending the treatment above the sill ensures that the drape does not interfere with the dressing table below.

Treating an Arch

Both valance and drapery styles can be made to conform to an arch shape. If you're hiring someone to custom-design an arch window treatment, expect to pay more since these styles take considerable time to plan and cut.

▶ A GOOD RULE OF THUMB in sizing valances is to highlight beautiful architectural details such as wide moldings whenever possible. The gathered balloon valances with generous poufed areas fit snugly within the molding of these oversized arch windows.

▲ THE INNER EDGE of the bold print fabric is highlighted with a contrasting print, adding an element of interest to this swagged window design. The rosettes add definition and are strategically placed to help form the swags around the arch.

▲ THESE GRACEFUL SHEER-FABRIC PANELS open in the middle to reveal the decorative leaded-glass window. By using Velcro® strips to adhere the fabric to the lip of the window molding, this look is simple to create. Bunching the fabric into rounded rosettes and puddling the fabric on the ledge helps to correct any length variations.

▲ YOU MAY BE TEMPTED to skip treatments on windows with panoramic vistas; however, the touch of color and style add character to the setting. The relaxed lower edges of these toppers soften the angular lines of the kitchen and maximize the view.

► FLANKING BOTH SIDES of the bookcase, these well-dressed windows feature a variation of a pulled-up valance. Repeating stripes are hidden in the side pleats while a broad stripe takes center stage and borders the sides.

It's a Cinch

A cinch valance is made from a rectangle of fabric that is pulled up or "cinched" at intervals across the width. Where you "cinch" the valance can change the look from a wide sweeping treatment to a balloon variety with proportional scalloped areas. The cinching is accomplished with the use of shirring tape or small plastic rings stitched to the back of the valance and threaded with Roman-shade cording. Shirring tape is a timesaver—the tape houses one or two cords that are pulled up to gather the valance once the tape is stitched to the back. Designer tassels or matching ties can be looped around the gathered areas to add a decorative touch.

▲ **THIS KITCHEN SINK** window is in a high-activity zone with a cinched valance that combines function and style. The beauty of a cinch valance is that the shirring tape can be adjusted to achieve the valance depth you desire.

▲ **MANY ROOMS HAVE WINDOWS** of varying sizes that can often go undetected when all treatments have a unifying theme. The side window on this porch has two scallops as a way to subtly differentiate it from the adjacent wall of windows.

CREATING CINCHING

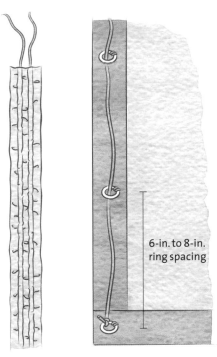

6-in. to 8-in. ring spacing

Shirring tape

Know Your Trims

Here's a handy guide to help you pair the right trim with your window treatment style and fabric.

BRAID TRIM

BALL TRIM

TASSEL TRIM

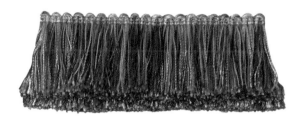

BRUSH TRIM

BULLION TRIM

BEAD TRIM

▲ THE MOST POPULAR variety of trim is the tassel, which can be made up of mini tassels for a delicate appearance or larger tassels for ornate decorator looks. The tassels look playful with the sun streaming through and provide a luxurious feel when teamed with a rich fabric, like silk.

Little Girl's Room

Deciding on window fashions for the little love in your life can get your creative juices flowing. Start by selecting a fabric that includes her favorite color, and then coordinate the walls, furnishings, and accessories. Window toppers add artistic flair. They can easily be layered over privacy blinds or panels, which can be closed at night to keep her feeling safe and cozy.

▶ A PAPER DOLL PRINT sets the stage for this delightful room. The unexpected yellow panels add a splash of sunshine to the setting and play off the minty green hue of the walls. Shocking pink banding ties both fabrics together while pastel-pink bead trim adds the crowning accent to an eye-popping treatment.

▲ PINK IS ALWAYS an irresistible choice for girls and looks best when presented in varying hues with a strong accent color such as green. This splashy garden-print fabric is softly gathered at the top edge and trimmed with ribbon bows. Matching drapery panels create an inviting setting for a tea party with a favorite bear.

▲ THE WHIMSICAL TRUMPET VALANCE, accented with bows, is purposely mounted at ceiling height to make the standard 8-ft.-high ceiling appear grander. The crown canopy over the bed acts as another window treatment would, bringing color and fun to this small room.

Gathered Classics

ADORNING A ROOM WITH VALANCES that are designed with ample fullness adds instant warmth and charm to the most basic of settings. Gathered toppers are often referred to as rod-pocket styles since most feature a stitched channel along the top edge to house a pole or curtain rod. Rod-pocket styles are easy to decorate with and can provide custom looks when properly lined and when edged with a fringe or cording. Print fabrics are especially well suited for gathered window treatment styles since the print can provide dramatic splashes of color in a room. For a professional look, shirring tape can be stitched to the back of the valance to create perfect pencil-like folds or a smocked look.

▲ AN EASY SOLUTION for a bay window is to hang gathered valances on rods installed end to end over the center and side windows. Leaving a ¾-in. space between mounted rods ensures that the rods can be slipped onto the hardware with little effort.

◀ A RUFFLED 2-IN. HEADER gracing the top of this elegant gathered balloon valance is further defined by a lower ruffle highlighted with contrast trim. The topper was mounted on a customized rod that angles forward at the center, adding dimension to the overall look.

◄ THIS COZY SITTING AREA features a boldly printed valance shirred onto a 2-in.-wide curtain rod mounted at ceiling height. The valance features three times fullness, meaning that the actual width of the treatment is three times that of the window, providing a more customized look.

▲ AN EMBROIDERED silk fabric adds high style to this simple trumpet swag topper. A petite tassel fringe, color coordinated to match the flocking in the silk, adds a delicate touch to the lower edge.

What Is a Header?

The fabric that extends above the rod pocket is called the "header," and this simple feature can alter the overall feel of a window treatment. As a general rule, the taller the header, the more romantic and feminine the look will be. Wide headers, 3 in. or more tall, can randomly flop forward if lined in contrast fabric, adding design interest to the top edge. Narrow 1-in. or 2-in. headers give valances a more classic, less fussy appearance than a wide header and work well if the rod pocket is sized for a 1-in. curtain rod or pole. The absence of a header provides a streamlined and sophisticated look, especially when the valance features an ample rod pocket for a 2-in.-wide curtain rod or pole.

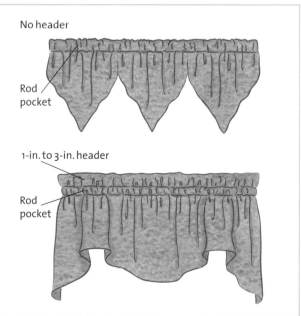

No header

Rod pocket

1-in. to 3-in. header

Rod pocket

▲ UNITE MULTIPLE WINDOW SHAPES within a room by using the same style valance and panels and hardware. Here, a playful valance formed from a simple rectangle of fabric is gathered into bell shapes along the upper edge of each window. While the arch window ends at the plant ledge, the skirt-style café curtains provide the illusion that the window is longer.

CHALLENGE: Gathered Arch-Top Valance

Traditional rectangular windows in this kitchen were treated with valances, and the homeowner wanted to treat this arch-top Palladian window in a similar way.

SOLUTION: Using the same fabric, trim, and style featured on the other windows, this arch-shaped valance was cut to fit the curve of the arch, highlighting the architectural elegance of the window.

▶ MOUNTING THE VALANCE along the ceiling line allows for maximum glass exposure. The center depth of the valance measures about 10 in., which is about the shortest length possible for a valance while still maintaining proper proportion.

▲ MANY KITCHENS FEATURE a bay-shaped eating area connected to the work center. The same window treatment style can easily unify the windows; the straight-edge valance here carries the line along the whole space, making the eye see the separate areas as one.

▲ THIS WINDOW SEAT fits perfectly in this room due to the addition of a straight-edge valance brought to life in a bold navy-and-white print. The valance offers enough color and dimension to the room without compromising the person relaxing on the seat.

Graceful Swagged Styles

By far one of the most popular window covering styles, swags have graced the windows of many fine homes throughout the world for centuries. Many of these tasteful fashions are adaptations of window dressings from as early as the Victorian era. In fact, many of today's top interior decorators find inspiration in history books when designing swagged window fashions for their clients.

Simply speaking, the swag is the crescent-shaped part of the treatment that gracefully sweeps across the window. Swags take on a formal look when paired with jabots, the fabric that adorns the sides of many swag treatments. Jabots are often referred to as cascades or tails, and shortened versions are sometimes placed between multiple swags to fill the space where they intersect. Adding special touches such as rich, tassel- or bullion-fringe trim to the swag and jabot edges elevates an ordinary swag to designer status. Traditional swagged styles can be toned down into informal, more relaxed looks when casually folded or draped across an interesting pole. Even a scarf swag, a simple length of fabric looped through one of the many interesting swag holders available, can soften an angular room with its sweeping style.

◄ AN EXPANSIVE WINDOW SEAT is cloaked in cottage charm with a trumpet swag detailed with button rosettes. The absence of a large curtain rod saved the homeowner money while allowing the swags to be a focal point. The swags are mounted on simple blocks of wood hidden beneath each trumpet.

New Takes on Traditional

TODAY'S SWAGS CAN TAKE ON MANY different looks yet remain elegant and regal—all it takes is a bit of knowledge when it comes to selecting the right style and fabric. The basic swag is a time-honored style featuring single or multiple crescent-shaped pieces flanked by side jabots or side drapes. It can bring old world charm to a room when made of one of the new silks or faux-silk fabrics. A new twist on the classic swag is the trumpet swag, with separate cone-shaped fabric "trumpets" positioned between swags that may fold open to reveal a contrast fabric. While most swag treatments are stapled onto mounting boards, pole swags are gracefully draped over a striking wood or iron pole, providing a lighter look while still adding a grand element of design to the setting.

▲ THE TEXTURE AND LUXURIOUS SHEEN of pure silk is striking in this traditional swag. The center swag is cut wider than the others to create impact while the tassel trim adds a less formal, more playful accent. Short side jabots cover the curtain rod that houses the drapery panels.

▶ A CORNICE-TOPPED trumpet swag adds style to this bathroom where the creative design details can be appreciated up close. The swag and jabots were mounted on a 1-in. by 3-in. board with rope-style piping concealing the line where the cornice sits on top of the swag board.

▲ THREE WINDOWS ARE ARTFULLY united in this transom bay setting by swags extending across each window to the angled corner. Folded side and center jabots disguise the high points where the swag ends meet. The contrast drapery fabric is repeated in the top layer of the center jabots, helping to unify the treatment.

◄ BLACK IS USED as a color accent throughout this area. The look of the soft white crepe swag is dramatically boosted by an exotic black trim with extra long tassels. The trim outlines the stately curves of the swags, creating a moving line in the room.

Anatomy of a Swag and Jabot

A single swag and jabot window treatment consists of three parts—one center swag and two side jabots (pronounced ja-bows). A swag is made from a piece of fabric that is cut into a modified evergreen tree shape. The swag is folded from bottom to top, bringing the angled edges together at the sides to create equal-sized folds, forming the crescent or U-shaped swag curve. The side jabots feature long angled edges and when folded, they reveal the lining fabric.

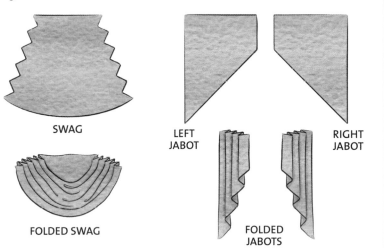

SWAG

FOLDED SWAG

LEFT JABOT

RIGHT JABOT

FOLDED JABOTS

◄ MOUNTED AT THE CEILING'S EDGE to expose as much of the view as possible, these multiple swags provide fluid movement across the window. The gently pulled-back side panels add a vertical line at the window's edge.

CREATIVE SOLUTION

CHALLENGE: Swags on an Arch Window

An arch-top triple window is difficult to decorate, especially with other, traditional-style windows in the room.

SOLUTION: A swag treatment was created to enhance the lines of this window and make it more of a focal point in the room. Inexpensive swag holders, available at home centers, were mounted high above the center arch and at opposite corners of the window. A fan-folded length of fabric is draped over the swag holders, creating wide graceful swags, and the excess fabric at both sides of the window is tucked under on the floor, creating a puddle effect. A tastefully designed bell of fabric highlighted with a coordinating check on the lower band serves as a central focus above the arch and also hides a bare spot on the wall. Corded rosettes intertwined with both fabrics provide just the right finishing touch.

   The side window style is completely different yet complements the arch window swag because of the swag shape on the lower edge and the height at which it is mounted.

▲ IN THIS TREATMENT, the jabots are a secondary element by their position beneath the continuous row of overlapping swags, yet they frame the view out the window. The curved line of the swags mimics the wide decorative arches above the window.

Jabot Placement

Jabot placement on a swag treatment affects the overall finished look.

JABOTS ON TOP OF SWAG: Mount jabots on top of the swag when you want them to stand out as a prominent design feature. Lining the jabots in a striking contrast fabric allows splashes of another color or print to show in the folds. For further definition, outline the edges with a coordinating trim or contrast band. Since the swag will be partially hidden, keep the finished width of each folded Jabot on the front of the board to 10 In. or less.

JABOTS BENEATH SWAG: Jabots beneath the swag allows the swag to become the primary focus of the window treatment; it also allows the continuous curved swag shape to help soften angular lines within a room. For multiple swags, remember the rule of odds: Three swags are better than two, and the center swag can be positioned on top or beneath side swags.

JABOTS ON TOP OF SWAG   JABOTS BENEATH SWAGS

◄ THE EYE-CATCHING JABOTS mounted on top of these swags form a zigzag line effect, adding overall interest to the treatment. If the jabots had been lined in the striped fabric, they would have faded into the side panels, and the center contrast swag would have become the central focus. As is, the jabots add balance to the treatment.

▲ THE SWAG AND JABOT TREATMENTS designed for each window within this bay area allow the handsome window moldings to show. Lace cafés, a casual addition to the more formal top treatment, were gathered onto simple sash rods to add intimacy to the setting.

How Many Swags?

- For windows up to 44 in. wide, use one swag.

- For windows up to 50 in. wide, you can still use one swag, but to avoid a stretched look, mount jabots on top to hide the extended width of the swag.

- Double windows divided with center molding look best with three swags.

- Triple windows may feature three or more swags, but plan on an odd number of swags for the best symmetry.

- Multiple swags that are 36 in. to 46 in. wide provide a grand, sweeping effect across a wall of windows.

- Multiple smaller swags, 25 in. to 35 in. wide, appear repetitious on large scale windows yet the look works if the room décor is simple and uncluttered.

▲ A LAKESIDE WALL of transom windows is enhanced with smaller-scale swags designed to follow the lines of each window. Alternating the swags by placing one in front and one in back makes a bold statement in a room where the décor is sparse and clean.

▲ A DRAMATIC ROOM with formal furnishings calls for an elegant swag treatment to tie the room elements together. The wide swags span two windows each, and the burgundy cording forms a design line that softens the rectangular shape of the transom windows below. The side drapery panels anchor the swags, providing balance to the look.

◄ MOUNTING THIS SWAG TREATMENT below the transom lowers the curved design line, making the swags an integral part of the living area below. The wide jabots help define each set of windows.

TRUMPET SWAGS

▲ THESE STRIPED FABRICS are combined in un-expected ways. The blue-and-white shirting stripe provides the subtle backdrop for an eye catching red-and-white stripe used for trim. The valance was positioned so it wouldn't interfere with the operation of the French doors.

▶ THIS TRUMPET SWAG treatment was placed high over these triple windows to optimize the view and elongate the windows. The extra-wide drapery panels cover wall space, too, adding an illusion of width.

Working with Stripes

Fabrics featuring even stripes, where the color bars on each side of a predominant stripe are the same, work best for swag treatments, since the color bars will appear evenly across the treatment.

Fabrics with uneven stripes, where the color bars are not the same on each side of a dominant stripe, are tricky to work with because the stripes will appear randomly. Plan for the center of each swag to feature the same stripe—select a dominant stripe if you want bold lines to appear across a treatment or a less-obvious stripe if you want to minimize the look of the bolder stripes. For the trumpets, place the same stripe in the center of each, preferably a different stripe than featured in the swag for a more interesting look.

▲ UNEVEN STRIPES ARE randomly displayed across these swags, but since they're narrow, their uneven appearance is minimized.

◀ A BOLD, PREDOMINANT STRIPE was placed in the center of each swag to tie the wall color into the window dressing. The thin stripe centered on each trumpet adds a precise touch.

POLE SWAGS

▲ TO ENSURE THAT THE GRAND PIANO remains the focal point of this formal music room, a cream fabric was chosen so that the pole swag treatment fades into the background. Rosettes made from the same fabric were tacked on to the ends of the pole, anchoring the panels and adding a touch of elegance.

▲ AT FIRST GLANCE, this pole swag appears to be one piece of fabric continually looped over the pole, but the swags and end panels were made individually and then stapled to the pole back. The soft green roping was draped in place after the swags were installed.

▶ SHEER PANELS WERE GATHERED on this pole for privacy. Then asymmetric swags were attached, with one long cascading panel tied into a French knot at the top of the pole on opposite sides. The narrow stripe featured as the bias banding adds a crowning creative element.

Mounting Swags in a Bay

1. Cut the center mounting board 2 in. narrower than the width between the corners of the center window opening.

2. Hold the side mounting board up to the side window at the same height as the center mounting board, leaving ¾ in. between board ends, and mark and cut the opposite end of the board at the side window molding or at the desired end point on the wall.

3. Mount the swags by stapling one to each board, wrapping and stapling the sides around the ends.

4. Staple the trumpets to the ends of the center board with half of each trumpet extending beyond the board ends. Staple the jabots in place by wrapping the sides around the ends.

5. With a hot steam iron press the gathers and folds down flat on top of each mounting board for a smoother look.

6. Install the treatment by screwing angle irons beneath the boards into the wall or by screwing the boards directly into the ceiling or soffit of the bay.

▲ **WHEN THERE IS A CEILING** or soffit above a bay window, mount swags at ceiling height to allow as much of the window to show as possible, for maximum light. Here, the stunning border and the brightly hued contrast fabric showing in the jabot folds frame the entire treatment.

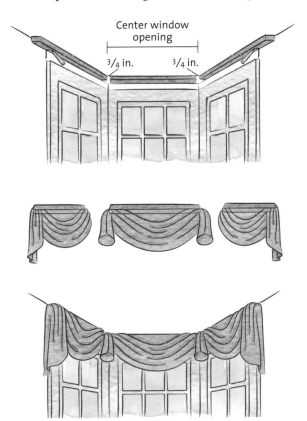

▲ **DECORATIVE TASSEL-FRINGE TRIM** added to the bottom edge of this treatment defines and enhances the seven different pieces that make up the bay window swag.

▲ **A CIRCUS TENT-INSPIRED STRIPE** makes a dramatic color splash as the broad stripes span out across the swags. This fabric ensures that the window treatments are focal points in the room, especially since they are contrasted by buttery yellow walls.

Asymmetric Swags

Swags are often shown in asymmetric styles, meaning the sides of the jabots end at differing lengths. This style works exceptionally well in rectangular rooms with little architectural interest. Sometimes asymmetric styles exhibit one side without a jabot or side panel at all—a good design trick if the window flanks a fireplace, bookcase, or other obstruction. Try this style on corner windows, leaving the sides closest to the corners untreated, or when two identical windows appear on the same wall.

▶ **FACED WITH A BOXY** living room featuring two front windows, this homeowner decided to make a statement with an asymmetric swag. The two-tone effect of the swag and panels works—as the swag fades into the wall color while the silky green panels pull forward into the room.

◀ **A HANDSOME BEADED-BRUSH** trim accentuates the edges of this regal pole swag and forms interesting lines on the intricate side jabots. The shorter jabots allow the elaborate wood paneling to show and draw attention to the sitting area.

Relaxed and Informal

AS OUR HOMES BECOME MORE CASUAL we want window treatments to follow suit. But that doesn't mean they can't be innovative and inspirational. Swags are very adaptable, and the gentle curves they offer a room can noticeably transform a cold, austere setting into a delightfully inviting one.

Relaxed swag looks can be achieved in several ways. The first has to do with shape—a swag can be rearranged to hang from decorative knobs or hooks, or be pulled upward in the center to create a whole new shape. Another way to revamp this elementary style is with the use of fabric, trim, and contrast banding. Casual cotton prints and no-fuss textures lend themselves to informal styles. Simple trims and braids in natural fibers such as jute also help enhance the treatment.

▲ THE LIGHTHEARTED FEEL of this hook-on swag began with the fabric choice—a botanical print reminiscent of the cutting garden outside the bank of kitchen windows. The hooks were positioned high enough on the wall so that the moldings wouldn't show above the swag when folded.

▶ A CASUAL POLE SWAG sets the tone for this family room and was an easy solution for the sweeping arch window. The large window would have felt bare—and the room a bit cold—without the swag adding color and movement.

Swags in the Kitchen

The kitchen windows are usually the first in the house to be decorated, mainly because we live in the kitchen the most. If you're starting from scratch in the kitchen, and swags appeal to you, here's a good plan of action:

- Pick a fabric you love, with all of your favorite colors.

- Next, select a coordinate or trim to help highlight the fabric. Use these accents throughout the room to tie the window treatments into the setting.

- Decide if you need privacy shades to minimize sun glare or to close out the world. Woven woods or Roman shades are great choices.

- Choose interesting hardware for mounting swag styles. Decorative door or cabinet knobs in interesting finishes can become fun design elements in the room.

▲ ROMAN SHADES ALONE in this kitchen would have made the stove be the primary focal point. Instead, the addition of floral print trumpet swags and red button rosettes make the whole space more lively by bringing more color into the room.

▲ A MINIMAL LOOK WAS USED for this panoramic span of windows, enhancing the view into the owner's private gardens. While the fabric is a floral, the soft colors and hues match the wall and cabinet tones in the kitchen allowing the swags to recede into the setting.

Swags Made Simple

Using individual swags in creative ways brings custom style to the kitchen sink windows at right. This is a great way to decorate transom windows in any room—it provides just a touch of fabric over each window while still allowing daylight in.

- Find a sewing pattern for the swag style you desire. Sometimes commercial patterns show individual swags hanging on top of drapery panels.

- To ensure that the swag fits your window properly, cut a sample swag from an old sheet or piece of scrap fabric and tape or thumbtack the swag over the window. The swag can be made larger or smaller by adding to or decreasing the size in the center of the swag pattern.

- QUICK TIP: Machine-stitch a hair elastic to the top of the swag on both sides. Loop elastics over installed hooks or knobs, tightening elastic by tying a knot in the excess. Arrange swag folds and enjoy!

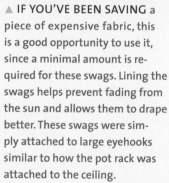

▲ IF YOU'VE BEEN SAVING a piece of expensive fabric, this is a good opportunity to use it, since a minimal amount is required for these swags. Lining the swags helps prevent fading from the sun and allows them to drape better. These swags were simply attached to large eyehooks similar to how the pot rack was attached to the ceiling.

◄ HANGING INDIVIDUAL SWAGS from a pole mounted over the transoms allows this patio door to open freely, and the long panels at the ends of the windows hide more of the glass. The privacy sheers mounted at door height can be pulled together when the sun sets—a perfect combination of treatments.

Changing the Window's Shape

When windows appear ordinary, a simple trick designers use is to alter the shape of the window by elevating the center of a treatment onto the wall above. This provides the illusion of a different shape breaking the repetitive pattern of straight lines in the room. Raising the treatment once in the center works well for single and double windows, but for triple windows you may want to raise the treatment twice along the top edge to keep it in scale with the wider width. Adding decorative details such as covered buttons on a trumpet swag draws the eye upward, especially when they're made from contrasting fabric.

▶ A SIMPLE SWAG CUT for a rectangular window is elevated in the center to provide an illusion of height on a squat kitchen window.

▶ WHEN THERE ARE MANY PATTERNS in a room already, introducing a solid or more neutral fabric at the window has a calming effect on a room's décor.

► THE WINDOW IN THIS dining room is unusually long and narrow. Drapery panels that stack onto the walls make the window appear wider and more proportionate to its length.

▼ A PICTURE WINDOW in this kitchen eating area needed a top treatment to act as a focal point at the end of this long room. A classic swag and jabot treatment, with three swags to reflect the windows below, helps to tie the décor elements together.

Corner Windows

Windows that are positioned in corners pose special challenges due to their close proximity to each other and to the corner. These windows can be treated in two ways: separately or as one window. If the windows stand alone with space between the molding and corner, you may choose two separate window treatments, but plan to have the sides of each treatment touch in the corner. Treating the windows as one unit is often a pleasing solution as the continuous appearance of the treatment makes the windows appear larger than they actually are.

▶ SINCE THE WINDOW TRIM of these corner windows touch, the best solution was to treat the unit as one piece. Draping swags into the corner also draws the eye to the stunning seaside.

▲ WITHOUT THE TRUMPET SWAG VALANCES, the windows in this corner sink nook would appear short and boxy. Mounting the treatments high on the wall allows for the side cascades to end well below the middle of the window, giving the illusion of height.

▶ ALLOWING SIDE JABOT TAILS to almost touch in the corner fills blank wall space and finishes off the ends of each trumpet swag treatment. Without the tails, this corner would have looked barren.

Decorative Knobs and Holders

Common hardware such as doorknobs, cabinet pulls, and tieback holders can be used to hold a valance in place while providing accents to a window. Knobs and pulls are available in a variety of sizes and materials, such as wrought iron, polished nickel, copper, glass, and wood. Installing them is easy with special screws threaded at both ends so the screw can be secured into the wall and the knob. Tieback holders, designed to secure draperies at the side of a window, also can be used at the top of a window and are often larger, providing a more substantial look.

▶ **LOOK FOR INTERESTING HARDWARE** at home centers, in catalogs, and online. Some of the best vintage finds can be discovered at flea markets and tag sales, and the price may be less than buying new.

▼ **GRACEFUL SCARF SWAGS** take shape when fabric is artfully folded and placed over brass tieback holders secured inside the window molding. The circular holders mirror the corner medallions in the trimwork.

▼ AN EASY-TO-MAKE kitchen valance is suspended from antique drawer pulls, which complement the color and simplicity of this swag treatment. A rod or pole would have been difficult to fit in the small space between the cabinets.

▲ USING DECORATIVE KNOBS in a bay window makes installing a swag treatment easy. Here, positioning the hardware at the top corners of each window works well, with a smaller swag positioned on the wall to hide the side drapery rod.

▼ STORE-BOUGHT SHEERS draped over decorative tieback holders provided an inexpensive solution for this wall of doors. The sheers add warmth to the room without disrupting the panoramic view.

Fabric Shades

Fabric shades offer the most value when it comes to window decorating. Not only can shades be aesthetically pleasing, allowing a radiant print or textured fabric to shine as a major focal point in a room, but they also serve the dual purpose of providing privacy when needed and shelter from heat or cold. Stylish shades can be easily suited for most room settings, appearing formal or casual depending upon fabric choice. Select a sumptuous silk and add a row of sparkling, beaded trim along the bottom edge for a rich, regal look, or choose a cheerful, colorful plaid for casual style.

If you're concerned about an expanse of fabric once a shade is lowered, the water-fall, or hobbled, shade is a fitting choice since the folds remain intact whether the shade is up or down. Billowy balloon shades add a touch of romance at the window, even when lowered. Adding innovative details such as fabric banding or ribbon trim will enhance the design effect of basic styles such as Roman shades. Or the shape of the bottom edge can be changed to provide a welcome break to the angular lines of rectangular rooms.

◄ SOFT WHITE ROLL-UP SHADES in this dining area are tied at staggered heights, providing an interesting backdrop for the beautiful table setting below. A cardboard tube, dowel, or PVC pipe is inserted into the lower edge of each shade, helping create the rolled effect.

Roman Shades

THE ROMAN SHADE has become a decorating staple since it is both useful and ornamental, especially when made up in one of the many gorgeous fabrics available today. Neatly stacked folds form at the bottom edge when the shade is raised, and when lowered, the shade lies flat against the window, offering protection from the elements and privacy from the outdoors. Numerous design enhancements can be made to basic Roman shades to provide decorating punch in a room. For example, add trim, a fabric band, or folds or tucks across the shade so it's interesting to look at when lowered.

When looking for softness at the window, balloon shades with fullness provide beauty and functionality. Roman shades also are easily combined with other window treatments, such as drapery panels or valances, creating a privacy option with flair.

▲ A BATHROOM IS TRANSFORMED into an elegant dressing area when luxurious silk is combined with balloon-shade styling. The lustrous sheen of the aqua silk makes this casual shade style dressier, fitting for this formal powder room.

▼ EXTRA-WIDE ROMAN SHADES unite a span of windows in this tropical theme guestroom. Pin tucks stitched across the shades provide horizontal lines around the room and add dimension, helping the eye work around the whole space.

▲ FRENCH DOORS are a welcome addition to any room but can pose privacy concerns. Hobbled shades that fall into cascading folds whether raised or lowered were mounted directly on each door to help close off this room when needed.

◄ THE CONTRAST of chocolate-colored walls, wide white trim, and brilliant red plaid provides splashy interest in this bedroom. The simple fabric roller shades can be whisked up to any position on the window, allowing for maximum daylight or total darkness.

▶ A TRIO OF WINDOWS is hidden behind three sets of drapery panels mounted on the same bamboo rod. Roman shades in a matching print were installed at pole height to mask empty wall space beneath the pole. Using the same fabric for all treatments adds a cohesive look to the windows.

Combining Style and Function

Roman shades make good companions for long drapery panels. The shade provides an attractive touch in the middle of the window and can be lowered for privacy; the stationary panels serve as decorative columns framing the window. This combination can be used as a decorating trick to camouflage small windows, since the drapery panels hide blank wall space, widening and lengthening the look of the window. By selecting coordinating fabrics for the shade and panels, additional design interest is created and the window becomes a focal point. Conversely, selecting the same fabric for both treatments provides a continuous look that helps to unify individual windows.

▶ COMBINING A ROMAN SHADE in a taupe-and-black check with striped linen panels creates a widening effect on a set of narrow French transom windows. The stationary panels make the window appear larger, allowing it to be a focal point whether the shade is lowered or not.

◄ ONE SET OF PANELS flanks the outer edges of two separate windows, uniting them as one. The crisp blue-and-white checked shades tie the room's color scheme together, and their relaxed shape fits the casual atmosphere.

▲ THE HOMEOWNERS WANTED to add fashionable yet functional treatments that would help reduce sun glare over the kitchen sink. Sheer linen Roman shades highlight each window, creating a stunning row of style. The shades also can be lowered separately, depending upon the position of the sun.

◄ THIS SOFT WHITE LINEN SHADE is pulled up to cover half of the window, allowing just enough light to filter through during the day. The tabbed panels mounted over the shade can be whisked closed if needed so the shade's position isn't changed.

▶ AN ENTICING WIN-
DOW SEAT was made
even more inviting with
the addition of swagged
Roman shades installed
end to end below the ceiling molding in the bay
area. The swooping effect
at the bottom edge of
each shade was created by
placing pleats 6 in. from
both sides, providing the
necessary fullness.

CHALLENGE: Fabric Shades in a Bay Window

This kitchen features an enormous wall of windows that begins over
a counter area and ends with a large bay window in a dining area. The
homeowner wanted to maximize the view but add a more intimate
feel to the whole space.

SOLUTION: Crisp swagged Roman shades in a vivid green-and-
white check fit each window in the bay area, allowing for easy installation into the angles of the bay. Small 1-in. angle brackets were
installed just below the crown molding, allowing the shade boards
to be inserted between the molding and the brackets. While the bay
window shades can be raised or lowered individually, a continuous
shade was made for the countertop window for convenience when
the sun is bothersome. Here, all shades are purposely pulled up to
highlight the crossbar mullions in the windows.

▶ A SLOUCHED LOOK IS DISPLAYED along the bottom edge of a shade when
the cording is placed about 3 in. in from the sides on the shade back. When the
shade is raised, excess fabric at the sides falls downward, while the middle area
forms a delicate curve.

Inside or Outside Mount?

Shades are stapled to pine mounting boards that are attached to the wall or window frame with angle brackets. To decide whether to mount these treatments on the inside or outside of the window frame, consider the design and structure of the windows. If the window frame is plastic, mount shades on the outside so that screws can be anchored properly.

INSIDE MOUNT: A shade installed inside the window frame or molding enhances the look of elegant trimwork and provides a border effect around the shade. When mounting inside a window, be sure there is at least 1½ in. of depth inside the window frame so that a 1-in. shade board can be installed flush with the outer molding or wall. Your shade board should be cut ¼ in. shorter than the inside frame width for precise fitting.

OUTSIDE MOUNT: The shade is installed on the outside of the window molding on the wall. Making the shade at least

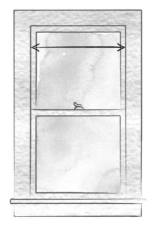
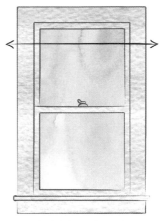

INSIDE MOUNT · OUTSIDE MOUNT

4 in. wider than the molding-to-molding measurement ensures that the shade will properly cover the entire window when closed. An outside-mounted shade looks best on a 2-in.-deep board so that the shade projects off the wall and clears any moldings comfortably.

◄ THE MOLDING AROUND this trio of windows nicely frames the inside-mounted shades, drawing attention to both the beautiful fabric and window trim. A matching shade mounted directly on the door was made slightly wider than the glass for sufficient coverage when closed.

▲ A BROAD, RECTANGULAR WINDOW above a whirlpool bath was treated with a tropical print Roman shade, bringing splashes of brilliant color to the room. The shade can be pulled up and down easily, as the window is only 40 in. long.

▲ THIS PLAIN, BOXY ALCOVE was revitalized with striking white canvas shades banded with navy fabric. The middle shade was cut to fit the width of the window, allowing wall space to appear to distinguish the center shade from those on the adjacent walls.

▲ TO DRESS A BAY-STYLE BATHING AREA like the one shown here, Roman shades were cut to fit over each window. When pulled to their highest position, these shades stack neatly, allowing the flirty ruffled edges to show.

How Wide Can a Shade Be?

Shades that are extra long and wide can be hard to raise and lower, which creates stress on the cording system over time. Use these guidelines for best results:

- Flat Roman shades can be made comfortably for windows up to 72 in. wide.

- Hobbled, or waterfall, shades featuring continuous folds are heavier when unfurled and work best on windows up to 60 in. wide.

- Shades that are relaxed at the bottom edge and feature one swoop when pulled up look best up to 60 in. wide.

- If using a blackout lining, the shade will be heavier and harder to pull up, so use a stronger cord.

- Shades for extra-wide windows can be made shorter than the window length. Less length means less weight on the drapery cording.

▼ EXTRA-WIDE SHADES meet end to end in this corner to create a continuous effect. These shades are swagged up several times to avoid one unattractive droop in the middle. This can be accomplished by adding cording in several evenly spaced places on the shades.

Fabric Considerations for Roman Shades

The flat surface and boxy style of Roman shades are a perfect place to display an unusual print or textured fabric. If selecting a toile scene or distinct print, estimate how much of the window will be covered when the shade is raised, then fit the print comfortably within this area and place the most visually pleasing motif in the center. Light to midweight sheers, silks, polyesters, jacquard weaves, and broadcloths work well for shades of all styles. Heavier upholstery fabrics and canvas also can be used as long as you keep to simple, flat shade styles.

▲ A SHEER ROMAN SHADE with pin tuck detailing adds a light and airy touch to this simplistic bathroom. The shade gently diffuses light during the day and can be unfurled at night for privacy.

▶ WHEN USING A SCENIC PRINT, it's important to plan your desired look accurately. The framed motifs in this fabric were purposefully placed in the top area of the shade, highlighting the distinctive designs.

Fabric Shades

All Roman shades feature a cording system on the back of the shade. By pulling the cords to various heights you can achieve different looks along the bottom edge.

▶ **THIS ROMAN SHADE** lies completely flat when lowered, allowing a beautiful print fabric to be highlighted. Vivid prints will become beacons in a room, drawing immediate attention to the windows.

▲ **KNOWN FOR THE RELAXED LOOK** of the folds along the bottom edge, slouched Roman shades should be several inches wider than the glass because the sides will pull in toward the window. For a sleek look, mount a white linen shade on a black iron pole with rings.

▶ **WHEN A HOBBLED,** or waterfall, shade is lowered, the folds remain in place, providing a cascading effect. The folds can be made small, as shown, or up to 8 in. deep for more contemporary styling.

▲ HOBBLED SHADES WERE MOUNTED at ceiling height to provide a flowing effect of folds down these windows. The fabric blends into the room, but doesn't dominate, allowing the fireplace to be the focal point.

▶ SHEERS ARE ALWAYS left unlined to allow light to filter through, which can emphasize a delicate print. A transparent ring tape was stitched to the back of this shade and cannot be seen through the sheer fabric.

Selecting the Right Lining

Not all linings are created equal. For lasting durability and performance of the shade, this is all you need to know:

- **DRAPERY LININGS:** Be sure to use a drapery lining that is sun- and rain-resistant to protect the decorator fabric from light and moisture damage. Most drapery linings are light-filtering, meaning that some light will show through. Dark, heavy fabrics will block the sun better than those lighter in color and weight.

- **BLACKOUT LININGS:** A blackout lining has a heavy, rubberized feel and can make holes appear on the shade where the cording rings are stitched. Look for one of the newer, softer blackout fabrics for better results. Hold the decorator fabric against a sample of blackout lining and up to the light to check for show-through.

- **INSULATED LININGS:** Specially made to block the elements, thermal linings help defray energy costs.

- **INTERLININGS:** If the decorator fabric is silk, the shade must be interlined with a mid- to heavyweight flannel to prevent the sun from fading and fraying the silk fibers. Interlinings are sandwiched between the decorator fabric and drapery lining.

▲ MOST FABRIC SHADES are lined with a midweight sun- and rain-resistant lining. This type of lining protects the decorator fabric from sun and moisture; however, some light will be able to filter through the shade.

▲ SINCE THIS UNLINED FABRIC SHADE allows the sun to blaze right through, the fabric colors will begin to fade within a short period of time. Backing shades with the proper drapery lining will help to preserve the treatment.

▲ WITH A BLACKOUT LINING, no light will show through this shade during daylight hours. The shade's color and appearance will remain the same at all times of the day since the sun cannot penetrate the lining.

▲ A BOLD, VERTICALLY STRIPED FABRIC makes a showy statement when featured in a flat Roman shade. Deciding which stripe to feature down the center of the shade will take some planning: try folding the fabric with different stripes placed in the middle to aid in the decision-making process.

Stripe Placement

Striped fabrics are especially well-suited for Roman shades, since the stripes can be fully extended down or across the shade to provide an interesting linear influence in a room. The bolder the stripe and the more it contrasts with the walls, the more stunning the effect. Placing stripes vertically along the length of a shade makes the window appear taller, as your eye is drawn up to the ceiling. Horizontal stripes make the eye sweep across a room and will give the window the illusion of being wider than it actually is. Be sure to plan for a pleasing stripe to be featured in the center of vertical shades or at the top edge for horizontal stripes.

▲ PLACING THE STRIPE HORIZONTALLY across a shade provides lively movement around this room and mimics the white stripes painted on the walls. The bold stripes in the shade and vivid picture frames advance into view while the cool wall colors recede into the background.

Striped Effects

Striped fabrics add dimension and character to all window treatments and can be paired with floral, plaid, or solid fabrics to create a textured and personalized look.

▶ **THE GREEN STRIPES WERE CENTERED** on each balloon section of this whimsical shade, with pink stripes peeking out at the sides. The combination of fabrics and the trump l'oeil painting makes this a welcoming guest room.

▲ **THE PLAYFUL COMBINATION** of a picket fence-inspired valance layered over a polka dot sheer shade provides a delightful touch to a narrow window. The shade valance was planned so that a bold stripe runs down the center of each picket.

▲ **THIS BEAUTIFUL DAMASK STRIPE** makes an eye-catching balloon shade. Although the stripes could not be placed evenly across the shade due to the pleating of the balloons, they were cleverly placed in the center of two balloons similarly. This allows the end stripes to fall where they may.

Hiding Hardware with Side Flaps

Outside-mounted shades, whether installed on a window or door, project out from the wall, allowing the eye to see the mounting brackets and cording from the side. To prevent this, fabric flaps made from the shade fabric can be stapled to the board ends to hide the hardware behind the board. The flaps should be 6 in. to 8 in. deep and can be made to fit the board end exactly or to be wider so that they wrap around the end, extending several inches beneath the shade on the front of the mounting board. Drapery weights can be placed in the bottom of the flap to hold it in place.

▶ THE EXPENSE OF ADDING FABRIC FLAPS to the board ends on custom-made shades is minimal. The flaps create a professional-looking shade that looks good when viewed from all directions.

▼ TO TAKE FULL ADVANTAGE of the view out these windows and doors, Roman shades in deep tan broadcloth are pulled up high. The ends of the shade boards are covered with fabric that appears to be another flap in the cascading effect.

▲ PETITE VALANCES, 4 in. to 8 in. deep, can be made for fabric shades, offering a clean, finished look at the top of the shade. The valance can also serve to hide the board ends and the hardware beneath.

◄ TREATING THESE WINDOWS separately would have drawn attention to their small, narrow shape. One wide Roman shade is mounted over both windows, uniting them for grander appeal.

CHALLENGE: Mounting Shades on Transom Windows

This sunny eating area features fantastic floor-to-ceiling transom windows and doors. Since the windows are the focal point, the homeowners wanted a minimal window treatment but one that would provide needed privacy in the evening.

SOLUTION: The homeowners enhanced the inherent beauty of the setting by mounting Roman shades inside the window frames, flush with the molding. The shades on the door were placed at the top edge of the glass for a continuous line. An off-white canvas fabric was selected to blend in with the setting, with green banding for a defining touch along the edges of the shades.

► IF THE SHADES HAD BEEN MOUNTED at the top of these windows, the handsome lines of the transoms would have been broken. The white shades offer design impact in a crisp, yet soothing way.

Roll Ups, Tie Ups, and More

Y OU WON'T HAVE TO LOOK HARD to find creatively inspired shade styles that offer decorative appeal while delivering privacy. Roll-up shades make a great choice for a child's room or casual living area; the simplistic styling might actually lure you into making the shade yourself. There are many tie-up options, too, all featuring a cording system that enables the shade to be pulled up into poufy balloons or swagged at the lower edge. Roller blinds, just like the old-fashioned white pull-up type, can be paired with a coordinating valance or set of side panels. For privacy at the lower half of the window, a bottom-up shade pulls to any height from the sill and acts much like a café curtain, giving a partial view. And don't forget about embellishments—beads, tassels, fabric bands, and braids can help customize even off-the-shelf shades to perfectly suit your tastes.

▶ A BALLOON SHADE serves as a decorative valance over a contrasting roller shade that can be whisked up or down as needed. Drapery cording threaded through plastic rings on the back of the balloon shade is tied in place to keep the shade stationary.

▶ THESE SIMPLE FABRIC roller blinds reveal a medallion of Battenberg lace. You can make your own by purchasing an inexpensive blind, removing the blind material, and stapling fabric fused with heavy interfacing onto the roller.

◄ A PLASTIC PVC PIPE in the bottom hem of a roll-up shade makes the shade easy to raise while revealing the contrasting lining. Roll-ups can be made as stationary valances with a blind hidden beneath for privacy if you don't want to roll the shade every day.

▼ THE RIGGING SYSTEM on this balloon shade allows the fabric to be pulled up at differing heights, creating an interesting look along the bottom edge. The sides are relaxed in contrast to the poufs formed in the middle of the shade.

► A SHORT, RECTANGULAR WINDOW becomes a striking asset to this room thanks to the simple white and tan fabrics chosen for the creative pull-up shade. Contrasting fabric bands stitched in place with matching bow-tie rosettes add a crowning touch.

Roll-Up Shade with Ties

You can make your own simple roll-up shade from items purchased at a local home center or fabric store.

1. **MATERIALS:** One sheer rod pocket panel to fit the inside width of the window plus 3 in. for side hems and the length of the window, plus 4 in. for bottom casing; one king-size pillow case in a contrasting color for the fabric ties; one suspension rod to fit the window width inside the molding; one 1-in.-dia. PVC pipe cut 1 in. less than the inside molding measurement.

2. **CUTTING AND STITCHING:** Cut the panel to the desired width and length, adding 3 in. for side hems and 4 in. to the length for the PVC pipe casing. Form side double hems by pressing the side edges to the back by 1½ in. then folding the raw edges in to the crease line; machine stitch ½ in. from both side edges. Form a pipe casing along the bottom edge by folding 4 in. back; press-fold in place and tuck the raw edge under by ½ in.; pin. Stitch close to the pinned edge. For ties, cut the pillow case into two 5-in. strips long enough to loop over the front and back of the shade as shown in the photo. Fold each tie in half, right sides together, and stitch one end and long side, using a ½-in. seam allowance. Turn, press flat, and slipstitch the ends closed. Insert PVC pipe into the bottom casing and slipstitch the ends closed.

3. **MOUNTING:** Cut the ends of the top rod pocket and dab the raw edges with seam sealant. Insert the rod; loop the ties over the rod evenly and suspend the rod securely in the window frame. Roll the bottom edge up to the desired height, knotting the ties in place.

Bottom-Up, Top-Down Roman Shade

A unique twist on the roman shade is the bottom-up version. These shades are installed the same as a regular shade, but by adding extra cords, they can be pulled up from the bottom or lowered down from the top to any height on the window. A small valance is mounted at the top of the window to hide the head rail that connects the shade to the top of the window. There must be at least 1 in. of space all around the inside of the window frame or molding in order to mount the shade properly. Bottom-up shades are popular in the bathroom or bedroom, where both privacy and a view are important.

▼ A HOBBLED WATERFALL SHADE pulls up from the bottom, covering the lower half of the window during the day. The shade can be pulled all the way to the top for complete privacy or raised to be completely hidden under the valance, exposing the entire window.

◄ BOTH THE POLE and the printed fabric contribute to the decorative effect of this tab-top Roman shade. A board is hidden behind the shade at the top of the window, holding the cording system that enables the shade to be raised and lowered.

▲ SOMETIMES IT'S THE SIMPLE DETAILS that give great impact. Here, the swagged bottom edge of sheer white shades are tastefully adorned with a delicate mini-fringe trim.

Trimming Shades

Add eye-catching appeal to an ordinary shade by stitching a row of decorative trim along the bottom edge, applying a striking ribbon or fabric band, or pulling up the bottom edge and adding a tassel as a focal point. Select a trim with a decorative lip that can be applied to the outside of the shade; the trim will provide more impact and can easily be machine-stitched or glued to the bottom edge. Bead and tassel trims work well, especially when a sun-catching material is used.

▲ TRIMS ACT AS STYLE CATALYSTS on window treatments and can be color coordinated with interesting items in the room, helping to tie a decorating scheme together. Without the trim, this relaxed Roman shade would have appeared ordinary.

▲ THE FLAT SURFACE OF THE SHADE is a perfect spot to highlight this garden-themed toile fabric; a centered tassel adds a creative spark and balance to the window.

◄ FABRIC BANDS IN A SLIGHTLY darker hue than the wall color outline the edges of these slouched shades. The short, boxy window could not accommodate drapery panels to match those featured on the side wall, so the shades tie the windows together.

Drapery Panels

Nothing beats fabric panels when it comes to adding instant warmth and style to a room, and today's drapery panels have been adapted to fit the way we live. No longer are draperies just considered for their function; panels are making high fashion statements in both formal and informal styles, and with new looks created in luxurious fabrics with texture, decorative trim, elegant rods, and accessories.

Creative elements are key. A visit to the window treatment aisle in your local home center will reveal a virtual explosion in the number of drapery rod and pole styles available. To complement new hardware, traditional drapery headings have evolved into sleek styles to include longer pleats with less folds or new goblet shapes. Basic panels can be attached to rods with extra-wide tabs cinched together with tassels, high-contrast ties, or even metal grommets. And when you want to pull the panels back to let the world in, there's an abundance of imaginative tiebacks available to fit your taste and budget.

◄ **EXQUISITE DRAPERY PANELS** were specially cut and folded to wrap around these arch windows, accentuating the beautiful curves. Tying the panels back high on the sides creates a flowing effect that ends in puddles on the floor, a foolproof trick used to avoid calculating an exact panel length.

Creating a Mood with Fabric Panels

WHEN FABRIC PANELS OUTLINE the edges of a window, the space becomes more comfortable and inviting. The fabric chosen should reflect the mood a room conveys. Lustrous silk reflects formality and enhances the richness of dark woods and silver accessories. Lush textures such as velvets and suede not only evoke feelings of grandeur but have insulating qualities, too. On the other hand, an embroidered sheer or textured linen conveys a sense of casualness, offering a relaxed, kick-off-the-shoes feel. When the drapery panels are meant to be the main attraction, opt for a splashy print, plaid, or stripe. If the panels are meant to serve a supporting role, a solid or subtle print that fades into the setting may be better.

▶ THE UNIQUE COMBINATION of French toile drapery panels set against the mahogany paneling lends charm to this library bay window. Using panels as stationary accents over the side windows prevents the vivid fabric from overwhelming the setting.

▶ IN THIS PERIOD HOME bathroom, the unexpected set of French doors are warmed with full-length sheer panels fashioned in earth tones for a bit of added privacy. The panels, with goblet-shaped pleats along the heading, provide an air of formality in the room.

▲ THE PINK TONES in these drapery panels are used throughout the room in the accessories, creating a high-spirited mood. The horizontal striped pattern of the silk panels adds fluid movement around the room.

◄ THIS FORMAL LIVING AREA is enhanced by the luxurious silk drapery panels. The mellow stripe in the silk blends with the wall color, providing a stately backdrop for the beautiful furnishings, which gain prominence as a result.

Making a Statement with Fabric

Drapery panels appear as large expanses of fabric in a room, so the fabric must be selected carefully for the right visual effect. Keep the following tips in mind while fabric shopping:

- Prints will look like splashes of color when the panel is gathered or pleated. In the store, scrunch the fabric together and view it from a distance to see how it will look in your home.

- Bold stripes can become lost when a panel is pushed open—the colors will randomly appear in the folds of the panel. Try the scrunch test in the store before buying this type of fabric as well.

- Prints with dark background colors, such as black, will make a statement and become immediate focal points in a room.

- The larger the print, the more attention the panels will receive. Toiles, floral prints, and plaids make excellent choices for drapery panels.

- Keep the scale of the room in mind when selecting print size. A flamboyant print can overwhelm a room with many windows. A small print may appear out of place in a large room.

▶ WITHOUT THE DARK LINES dividing the geometric shapes in these panels, the abstract pattern in the fabric would lack definition. The dark wood table in the room contrasts boldly with the fabric, and the floral chair introduces another pattern that works unexpectedly well here.

▲ WHITE CABINETRY PROVIDES the backdrop for the vivid conversational print fabric adorning this valance and sill-length panels. The bold hues in the fabric seem to move forward into the kitchen, drawing attention to the rich granite countertops.

◄ THE TWO FLOORS in this soaring front-hall foyer are unified with tightly gathered floor-to-ceiling drapery panels flanking the arch-style windows. The brilliant plaid provides a dramatic backdrop for the detailed trimwork and contrasts the soft white walls.

CHALLENGE: Transom Windows

The floor-to-ceiling arched transom window was a stunning focal point in this room, but its massive size seemed to dwarf the furnishings. The homeowner wanted to tie the seating area in with the window and also find a way to diffuse afternoon sunlight.

SOLUTION: A combination of different drapery panels is the key. To add a defining touch at the ends of the window, stationary panels in a bold floral help draw the eye down to the couch area. Sheer panels were installed on the same pole, which features a channel with clips that attach to the drape tops. This unique system allows panels to move along the pole without rings. The sheers also can be closed for sun glare protection or pulled open to maximize the view out the windows.

▲ IF YOU'VE INVESTED IN HIGH-END WINDOWS, the dressings should accentuate their architectural beauty. The color and print choice for these side draperies allows the panels to take on the supporting role of showcasing the magnificent window.

Ring-Top, Pleated, and Shirred Panels

IF YOU WANT TO ADD STYLE to a room quickly, ring-top panels offer handsome looks and are the most versatile of all drapery types. Since the panels are flat, drapery hooks or clip-on rings are installed evenly across the top edges, allowing for quick installation onto a decorative pole. The spacing between the rings influences the overall look; the farther apart they are, the more relaxed the finished look will be. For traditionalists, classic pinch-pleat headings can be modified in new ways, with longer pleats across the top of extra-long drapes helping to keep the treatment in scale with the window. If you're sewing your own drapes, you can achieve professional-looking results with relative ease by using new shirring tapes, which create perfect pencil pleats or a hand-smocked effect along the header.

▲ BY INSTALLING THE ROD 3 in. above the molding, there is room for the rings to suspend the drapes 1 in. above the trimwork. The beautiful molding is exposed, and the smocked heading on the drape is emphasized below the dark line of the wrought iron rod.

◄ FRENCH DOORS require clearance to ensure they can swing freely, so the rod was placed midway between the door molding and the ceiling trim. The rods above the windows were mounted at the same height to provide a continuous line around the room.

◄ A NO-PLEAT LOOK was cleverly engineered by placing pleats on the back of the drapery panel out of view. This enables the drape to stack neatly when opened and provides a sleek heading along the top of the panels.

Where to Mount a Pole

When planning to hang drapery panels, where to mount the hardware is the first question to address since rod placement determines panel length. For ring-top panels, keep in mind that drapery rings will lower the fabric from the rod by an inch or more, depending upon the size of the rings. Remember also to consider molding height and ceiling height. If you have wide trimwork, plan to mount the top of the pole even with the molding. For dramatic impact, mount the pole just below the ceiling's edge. This long, cascading effect can actually make the window look longer and the ceiling seem higher than they are.

Here are two other placement options to consider:

▪ SLIGHTLY ABOVE THE MOLDING: By mounting the rod 2 in. to 4 in. above the molding, you ensure that the glass will be completely covered by the fabric. When hanging ring-top panels, hold the rod with the rings attached over the window. The top of the drapery panel should begin at least 1 in. above the window molding or opening for best results.

▪ HALFWAY BETWEEN THE MOLDING AND CEILING: To elongate the look of your windows, mount the rod approximately half the distance between the window top and the ceiling. This will draw the eye upward and highlight the rod against the wall.

POLE HEIGHT VARIATIONS

Ceiling height

Halfway between molding and ceiling

Slightly above the molding

Molding height

► MATCHSTICK WOVEN-WOOD BLINDS were first installed inside this window molding for privacy. To dress the window to fit the room's ambience, the homeowner mounted simple rod-pocket panels at the sides of the window and then added triangle swags in a flat braid to blend the entire treatment with the blinds.

Layering Treatments

Adding a decorative topper over side drapes or mounting a privacy shade beneath drapery panels is a great way to combine form with function. Custom Roman shades are perfectly suited to layering with panels. Keep in mind that each treatment on the window needs space to extend out from the wall or molding. If possible, mount shades inside the window frame to make room for the drapery rod. For shades that must mount on the outside of the molding, position the top edge of the shade to fall behind the drapery pole. This hides the gap between the top of the shade board and the pole. Mounting the panels onto the wall makes the window appear wider.

◄ A TRIO OF WINDOW COVERINGS masks an ordinary set of windows. The blinds act as the privacy layer with a romantic balloon shade mounted on top. The ring-top panels extend onto the wall by a foot on each side, giving the windows a more expansive look.

Creative Pleats and Headings

The vast array of beautiful drapery poles, rings, and finials flooding the marketplace has spurred a creative revolution when it comes to drapery heading design. Forget traditional pinch pleats—today's drapes feature details along the top edges that draw attention the minute you walk in the door.

▶ **A SIMPLE FLAP OF FABRIC** added to the top of a flat panel is accentuated with a braid trim that forms a dividing line between the two layers. You can also forgo the flap and stitch braid directly to the drape for a quick mock-valance look.

▲ **ELEGANT GOBLET PLEATS,** with their characteristic champagne flute shape, are made from a drapery heading stiffened with buckram or heavyweight interfacing to help the pleats hold their shape. Filling each pleat with crumbled tissue paper is also a trick sometimes used for shape retention.

▲ **OFTEN REFERRED TO AS THE EURO,** or soft fold, pleat, three folds of fabric brought together and stitched at the top allow the fabric to drape casually into folds along the length of the panel. Tailored in appearance, this pleat has all but replaced the traditional pinch pleat.

SHEERS

▶ **SHEER PANELS WORK WELL** when a light, airy feeling is desired. Here, textured sheers can be drawn open in the daytime to reveal the beautiful view. Easily pulled closed on rings at night, they provide a sense of intimacy yet still allow moonlight to filter through.

▲ **SOMETIMES THE ONLY DRESSING** a window needs is a sheer, especially when the walls are painted a vivid hue. Nautical roping is cleverly laced through these panels and over the swing rods, bringing a three-dimensional element to the window.

▲ **THE LIGHT IN THIS SUNROOM** is gently diffused with ceiling-to-floor sheers while softening the harsh lines of the iron daybed. The brushed nickel rods form a border-like effect at the ceiling's edge, helping to pull the eye down into the room, creating a more intimate space.

Sheers on Transoms

A clever way to add warmth without hiding a beautiful transom window is to make a panel with sheer fabric inserts.

1. **PURCHASE THE PANELS:** For one set of finished panels, purchase two sheer panels and one fabric panel for the middle. All panels should be the same width. For a decorative accent, purchase cording in the amount of four times the width of one panel. Cording should have a lip to insert in the seams.

2. **CUT THE PANELS:** Install a drapery pole at the desired height. Hang sheers from rings and place pins at the points where you want the top and bottom sheer panels placed. To determine the length of the center fabric panel, first measure the distance between the pins on the sheer panels and add 1½ in. for seams. Cut two fabric panels to this measurement. Cut one sheer ¾ in. below the top pin and ¾ in. above the bottom pin, which allows for seams. Repeat for the remaining sheer panel.

3. **STITCH:** With the right sides of the fabrics together and using a ½-in. seam allowance, stitch the sheer panels to the top and bottom edges of the fabric panel, inserting cording in the seams if desired.

▶ **THIS CREATIVE WINDOW TREATMENT** allows light and privacy while highlighting, not hiding, the transom window. Although the treatment is made of three panels—sheer on top and bottom and fabric in the middle—the colors are from the same family and the combination is subdued, helping the fabric differences to blend harmoniously. The treatment is suspended from pearl beading typically used on bridal gowns.

Panel Length

Deciding where to end panels is often a matter of personal preference. Different looks can be achieved when the fabric is allowed to brush the floor or cascade into graceful folds. Consider these factors to help achieve the look that is just right for you:

- **SILL LENGTH:** Plan for shorter panels to fall at the sill or at the bottom of the window molding, not in the middle of wall space.

- **FLOOR LENGTH:** Panels should end approximately ½ in. above the floor for a smooth, custom look. Floor-length panels fall freely yet stay orderly and tidy—a good idea if you have small children.

- **BREAK LENGTH:** Adding 2 in. to the floor length allows panels to gently sweep the floor, creating a full design effect along the lower portion of the drapes.

- **PUDDLE LENGTH:** Adding 8 in. to 12 in. to the floor length creates the most relaxed feeling of all as the fabric forms a "puddle" as it fans out on the floor.

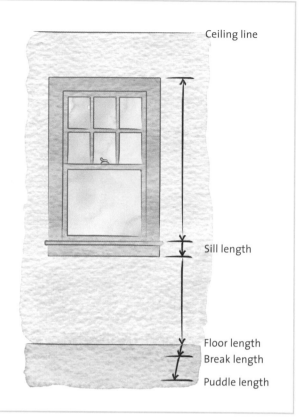

Ceiling line

Sill length

Floor length
Break length
Puddle length

▲ THE EXTRA FABRIC gracing the floor does not pose a hazard for little feet because the panels are tucked behind furniture and plants.

▶ THE PUDDLING EFFECT of these panels provides a voluminous look at the bottom edge. Stationary panels work best in this drape length since you can style the fabric as you want and then leave it alone.

▲ FAN PLEATS DECORATE the
top of these panels, which can be
whisked closed when needed. The top
edge is scalloped so that it dips down
between pleats. Ending the panels at
the bottom of the molding frames the
window precisely.

◀ PANELS THAT END slightly above
the floor add a feeling of perfection
to the room. Here, the trim at the bottom edge of the panels accentuates
their neat folds. They never need to be
touched since a privacy shade is
installed beneath.

DECORATIVE HARDWARE

▲ THE STEEL ROD for this bay window was custom made, but some home centers and specialty outlets also carry rods for hard-to-fit windows. Curved elbows were installed into the angled corners with rods then cut to fit.

▲ CREATE YOUR OWN custom-look pole for a wide expanse of windows by installing a decorative tieback holder above the center of the window, allowing the finials on the pole ends to touch the holder on each side. Such a detail becomes an instant focal point.

▲ A GLOSSY SILVER ROD was sized to fit perfectly inside the gable end of this bedroom. Accents of silver throughout this room, such as the beading along the headboard, reflect the finish of the rod, helping to tie the room together.

◄ BAMBOO RODS CONTRIBUTE to the natural feel here, especially since they're combined with woven-wood shades. The skinny metal rings holding the panels provide an interesting mix of textures, especially when repeated in the headboard.

Hardware Options

You don't have to look far to find spectacular drapery rods, poles, and finials to properly showcase your new fabric panels. Home centers, discount stores, and stores that carry decorator fabrics are filled with beautiful selections; even the Internet can be a great resource for one-of-a-kind looks. Professional decorators have access to many styles not available to the public. If you're searching for an extra-long rod or a wide-diameter pole, a professional decorator may be the best source.

Finials are the decorative knobs that attach to the ends of a pole or rod. Combining poles with finials in different colors or finishes is an interesting way to add a noteworthy touch to the window. When deciding on pole or rod and finial size, take into account the size of the room. Narrow rods placed over expansive windows will look meager compared to heavier poles and finials that are more in scale with the setting. Remember that the hardware you select is an investment in the window and is as important as the drapery style you plan to feature.

► WOOD POLES WITH BLACK ACCENTS and inlaid design features can be chosen to match similar furnishings within a room. Wrought iron is also a popular choice for drapery hardware and can be found in faux-iron materials that are less costly.

▲ POLES AND FINIALS can be found in numerous finishes. Matching the pole finish to the finial provides a continuous line along a window, while mixing finishes draws special emphasis to the finials. Tieback holders can combine several finishes, pulling a mixed pole and finial look together.

▶ A TRIPLE-WIDTH PANEL with contrast banding stacks all the way to the side wall, making room for the door to swing open. The expanse of fabric anchors the wall of doors, adding casual style to a walk-out living area.

Using Stack-back to Your Advantage

One of the greatest advantages of draperies is that the long stretches of fabric can provide visual illusions, making small windows or doors appear larger in height and width than they actually are. Stack-back, the amount of space a drape covers when pushed to one side, can be planned so that drapes stack off the window onto empty wall space, allowing all of the window or door glass to show.

STACK-BACK GUIDELINES

The optimal stack-back ranges for various widths of lined drapery panels made from medium-weight fabric are:

- 50-in. panel stack—10 in. to 15 in.
- 75-in. panel stack—13 in. to 20 in.
- 100-in. panel stack—18 in. to 25 in.
- 125-in. panel stack—23 in. to 30 in.
- 150-in. panel stack—28 in. to 35 in.

▲ OUTLINING MULTIPLE SETS of French doors with full drapery panels provides symmetry between the individual door units. Each rod, mounted above the detailed molding, was cut 2½ ft. wider than the door to allow for panel stack-back onto the wall. The doors not only appear wider but also longer.

▲ TAUPE SILK PANELS fashioned with inverted pleats along the heading stack way off the door, covering blank wall space. The panels provide the visual effect of a fabric-covered wall and serve as a striking backdrop.

▲ THE ROMAN SHADES on these doors provide privacy while the linen drapery panels can stack back to let in light or be pulled closed for instant warmth and intimacy.

CREATIVE SOLUTION

CHALLENGE: Doors in a Corner

The new owner of this house was delighted with the arch-top French doors but wanted window treatments that would make the room feel more intimate and add privacy at night.

SOLUTION: When doors or windows are placed in a corner, a window treatment can still be used. Here, a drapery pole was cut a foot wider than the window and installed just below the crown molding. One end of the pole features a finial while the opposite end is flush with the corner. A drapery panel with extra fullness stacks onto the wall along one side of the door, allowing for maximum glass exposure during the day. At night, the panel slides easily across the pole on rings.

▶ ANOTHER SOLUTION FOR THIS DOOR could have been to stack side panels that split in the middle along both sides of the door, although this would have compromised the view. Here, the white-on-white fabric and wall combination has a soothing effect in a room otherwise dominated by black tones.

GATHERED PANELS

▲ THE HARD LINES of this wood cornice are softened with extra-full panels of gauzy, sheer fabric gathered onto a rod beneath the board. The wide pieces of fabric are tied back at the sides, creating a stage curtain effect that showcases the window.

▲ A DECORATIVE SIDE PANEL is gathered on a simple curtain rod at the crown molding. A floppy 5-in. heading above the rod pocket is lined in a contrast fabric that shows in the folds along the top edge.

▶ GATHERED PANELS FOLLOW the shape of this arched doorway, drawing attention to the regal curve. Two rows of cording trim hold the gathers in place and provide visual interest along with rosettes spaced around the curve. The pair of tassels centered over the door adds a unique finishing touch.

STATIONARY PANELS

▲ THESE SIMPLE RING-MOUNTED stationary panels that extend only halfway over the side windows are intended to be decorative. The white fabric against the blue walls softens the windows and does not obstruct the view.

▲ SINGLE-WIDTH PANELS mounted above the transom windows throughout this sunroom draw the eye up to the richly painted ceiling. The skirt of contrasting fabric that folds down over the decorative rod is cinched together with a fabric band, creating an interesting fan-like effect.

◄ STATIONARY DRAPERY PANELS provide the background for elegant swags with flowing tails that are mounted on the same drapery pole. A benefit of decorative side panels is the expense factor—less fabric is needed since the panels do not close.

Tabs, Ties, and Grommets

ADDING TABS, TIES, OR GROMMETS to the top edge of simple draperies gives a unique look to an otherwise plain window treatment. Tab tops are no longer simple country-style curtains, especially when extra-large tabs are individually cinched together with decorative cording or napkin rings. Tying a panel onto a unique rod is another way to dramatically enhance a panel's look, especially when the ties are made out of contrasting fabric. For a more contemporary look, use sleek, oversized grommets at the tops of panels. While you may need to have a decorator or home décor shop professionally install grommets, the style is perfect for more masculine and minimal décor settings.

▶ FABRIC PANELS TIED to drapery poles draw attention to the birds and branches scene stenciled along the perimeter of the room. The soft green ties mimic the color of the leaves, becoming a part of the delightful display above.

▶ THIS UPSTAIRS HALLWAY was transformed into a back-to-nature vignette when the homeowners installed a custom drapery pole made from a stained dowel accented with twisting vines. The slouch-style drapery panels are tied onto the pole with only three ties, allowing deep casual pockets to form at each panel top.

◄ OVERSIZED GROMMETS large enough to accommodate a steel drapery rod allow panels to fall into neat, clean folds that complement the simple furnishings in this room. The color blocking was cleverly planned so that the dark gray fabric frames the door while the contrasting white sheer allows light through.

▼ FAN-TAB DRAPERIES take on relaxed style when the tabs are made 6 in. wide and pinched together with simple fabric bands. The drape top here was cut into a scalloped shape to allow the fullness to fall forward in a comfortable way, reflecting the ambience in the room.

Decorative Knobs and Pulls

Use your imagination when adding artistic styling to common drapery panels—doorknobs, kitchen and bathroom cabinet pulls, and even pole finials can be used to hang window panels.

▲ **AN ORDINARY BEDROOM** was creatively inspired by a golden damask drape suspended from artsy drawer pulls. Lining the drape in a contrasting stripe to match the taupe hue of the walls provides a touch of interest at the top and side of the panel.

▲ **A ROOM WITH DRAMATIC COLORS** and furnishings calls for a simple window treatment. This solution uses sheers bordered with a geometric pattern, hung from simple cabinet knobs. When many knobs are needed, it's best to keep them small to avoid overpowering the window treatment.

▲ **AN ASSORTMENT OF ECLECTIC** drapery holdbacks creates a stunning effect along the top of this corner window. The contrasting stripe cuff at the top of the drapery panel and matching tieback holder provide an additional color accent.

◄ AN ALCOVE FEATURING a sensational arch-style window has been custom-fit with wood shutters to allow light in the room. The stark look of the shuttered window is soothed by silky damask drapery panels mounted around the window on decorative tieback knobs.

CHALLENGE: Decorating Sliding Doors

A solarium in this 1960s home features multiple sets of sliding doors. The homeowner wanted to update the look of the room without investing in new doors.

SOLUTION: Refurbishing older homes can be costly, so sometimes it pays to work with the existing bones of a room by highlighting the good and downplaying the not-so-good. The walls here were painted a dark green to mask imperfections, and a silky, white polyester-blend fabric was chosen for the drapery panels to add lightness and warmth to the sliders. Drapery rod finials with a leafy motif were adapted to screw into the trimwork above the doors, enabling the fold-top drapery panels to be secured at ceiling height. The black bullion-fringe trim highlighting the layered edge of the drapes adds an interesting design line to the room and picks up on similarly colored accessories, such as the chandelier. Tying the panels back low on the doors brings the beautiful gardens into view.

▲ FINDING A NEW USE for drapery rod finials inspired the design of these striking drapery panels. Using white at the window is always soothing and serene; here it unifies the other white furnishings in the room.

Café Curtains

SOMETIMES THE BEST SOLUTION for windows that look out on a busy street or unwelcoming site are café panels. Cafés can be an integral design element when embellished with contrasting ribbon and buttons, or when shirred tightly onto a rod. Sometimes cafés are the only treatment on a window, and a look that works especially well on a window that features beautiful molding or an interesting shape at the top. Cafés also can be combined with a window topper made of the same fabric for a cohesive look in the kitchen, bathroom, or nursery. The light and airy feel of cafés, along their easy-open, easy-close functionality, make this a winning style.

▲ THIS SHEER CAFÉ measuring triple the window's width is gathered onto suspension rods that precisely fit the lower half of the window. Foregoing a heading along the top of the curtain gives the café a more sophisticated look.

▼ THE CRISP HANDKERCHIEF-LINEN CAFÉ adds intimacy to the rocking chair nook in this nursery. Tiny button tabs hold the delicate curtain in place with prancing horse ornaments installed whimsically across the rod.

▲ THEY'RE BEAUTIFUL, but these multiple arched windows created a fishbowl effect at night when the family was dining. The sheer cafés, mounted high on the window for privacy, have many custom features including a self ruffle and ribbon banding. Bright red buttons and rings tie the windows in with the décor.

◄ ADDING A GENEROUS amount of fabric above a rod pocket café lends an air of romance to the arch window in this French country–inspired workroom/laundry room. The printed gauze fabric mixes well with the décor and provides just the right touch of privacy.

New-Look Tiebacks

IF YOU'RE GRAPPLING WITH whether to leave drapery panels hanging straight at the window or pull them back, consider the design effect provided by a rope tassel or vintage tieback holder. Pulling drapes to the side creates a graceful curved line, a solution that makes sense in boxy spaces. Be inventive when selecting tiebacks. Men's ties lend a preppy look in the den, while drapery holdbacks made from baseballs cut in half are fun accents in a child's room.

When installing tiebacks, remember that their placement on the window affects the shape of the panels. Avoid centering a tieback in the middle of a panel, which would divide the window in two. More pleasing proportions can be attained when the drape is pulled back in the top half or lower half of the window.

▲ GORGEOUS YELLOW-AND-WHITE damask panels are tied back high on the windows, allowing maximum light into this colorful dining area. Simple matching fabric bands were chosen to hold the drapes in place, allowing other elements in the room to have prominence, such as the sparkling chandelier.

▲ WHEN A DRAPERY PANEL is tied back low on the window, the fabric above the tieback gives the window the illusion of being taller, providing greater visual impact. For rooms with numerous windows, be sure to place all tiebacks at the same height.

▲ THE CONSISTENT LOOK of this wallpaper and drapery fabric is purposely broken with the bright yellow fabric lining that is revealed when the drapery panels are tied back. The drapes form a gentle pouf where the tieback holds the fabric, adding a soft curved line.

▲ INVESTING IN UNIQUE or elaborate tiebacks can spruce up existing draperies or create stunning accents to newly installed panels. Your choice of tiebacks can either complement the drapery fabric to create a subtle highlight or contrast with the fabric for bolder eye-catching impact.

◄ BY TYING THESE DRAPERY panels in the top third of the window, a stately look is created, elongating the windows and allowing the furniture to stand out. Tasseled tiebacks are secured to the wall in line with the natural break of the window below the transom.

Quick and Easy How-To

There are many quick and easy window décor projects that can be completed in as little as one or two hours. The first step is to learn how to measure your windows. Then begin looking through patterns at fabric stores and on Web sites to see what will suit your needs. If you don't want to start from scratch, you can still add your personality by modifying ready-made panels or valances (found everywhere from discount stores to home centers and the internet) with trimmings and accents. From the creative planning process to the installation, you'll learn new tricks along the way, knowing soon you'll be able to sit back with pride as you enjoy your newly decorated windows.

◄ THIS ONE PIECE, NO-SEW SWAG was fashioned from yards of sateen fabric, uniting a wall of individual windows. The fabric was pulled through swag holders mounted just below the ceiling's edge, forming shallow swags between the poufy rosettes.

Ready, Set, Sew

SEWING YOUR OWN window treatments can save a significant amount of money compared to the cost of hiring a decorator or having items custom made. The designer fabrics available today provide endless options for beautifying your windows, and the wide selection of sewing patterns will help ensure stylish success. Remember, sewing window décor is easier than garments since windows are usually basic box shapes, and any imperfections can be disguised in the gathers, folds, or pleats of the treatment. Since you will be handling sizeable pieces of fabric, prepare by giving yourself a sufficient and comfortable work area such as a ping pong table or extended dining table.

▲ SINGLE TRIANGLES OF FABRIC tied end to end form an interesting shape along this picture window. When decorating large windows, selecting a sewing pattern that divides the window into individual pieces is always easier than making one large window treatment, especially if you're new to sewing.

▼ THIS SIMPLE VALANCE made from a rectangle of material uses a bold, eye-catching fabric design to create excitement. While the window at the end of the room is treated differently with drapery panels, a harmonious look still exists in the room because the same fabric and pole hardware was used.

What's New in Sewing Equipment

Whether you're returning to sewing or learning for the first time, you'll be amazed at the sophistication of sewing machines, accessories, and irons on the market. Sewing machines are now computerized, enabling you to sew a multitude of decorative stitches with the touch of a button or screen. Many have software programs that work through your personal computer, allowing you to apply professionally finished appliqués to your projects. You may also consider a serger, a machine that sews about 1,500 stitches per minute while cutting and overcasting edges at the same time. Although a regular machine is still needed for stitching into corners and top-stitching, the serger is fast and fun, especially on long expanses of fabric. New irons with continuous steam options generate clouds of steam from a separate water tank, helping to create a professionally pressed look. Special lamps also are available that provide true color, low-glare light that reduces eye strain.

▲ **A NEW GENERATION** of computerized sewing machines offers hundreds of stitch options, embroidery features, and stitch-regulating technology for uniform stitching. Sewing window treatments requires stitching over multiple layers of fabrics, so it's best to purchase a machine that can handle fabric volume.

▼ **A LIGHTWEIGHT STEAM** generator iron with a separate water tank provides hours of continuous steam on demand, a helpful feature when mounting window treatments. These irons also are well suited for everyday wrinkle removal.

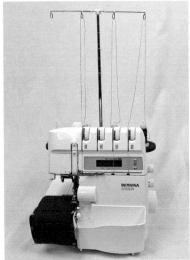

◄ **SERGERS COME IN** 3-, 4-, or 5-thread models. All sergers trim, stitch, and professionally finish seams while stitching up to ten times faster than traditional sewing machines. Look for an easy threading model that can perform the narrow rolled hem stitch for quick edge finishes.

◄ **FLOOR LAMPS WITH SPECIAL** white light technology are well suited for the sewing room, especially since they can be easily moved from cutting table to sewing machine. The true lighting shows colors and details clearly with low-heat, low-glare, soothing illumination.

Measuring Your Window

Even before buying fabric and a pattern, you need to measure your window and the surrounding area. Begin by using a retractable metal measuring tape for accuracy. Measure each window individually even if they appear to be the same size.

WINDOW WIDTH CONSIDERATIONS

A: For inside-mounted shades and valances, measure the width inside the window frame. Mounting boards should be cut ¼ in. less than the frame for a proper fit.

B: Outside-mounted shades and valances can feature a mounting board the same as the window width. Measure the width from the outside of each side of the molding. The mounting board should be secured to the window molding or just above.

C: Outside-mounted shades and valances can feature a mounting board or curtain rod wider than the window width. Add 4 in. to your window width measurement to enable the board or rod to be secured to the wall.

D: For drapery panels, extend the pole or rod out from the window molding to give the illusion of a larger window and to allow for stack-back of the panels on the wall. Measure the amount of stack-back desired (D) on one or both sides, and add it to window width (B) for your drapery rod bracket to bracket width. (See p. 154 for more on stack-back.)

WINDOW LENGTH CONSIDERATIONS

E: For inside-mounted shades or valances, measure the desired length inside the window frame.

F: For outside-mounted shades and valances, place the treatment 2 in. to 4 in. above the molding to allow more glass to show. The sides of a valance or jabot should extend down and stop in line with a horizontal fixture in the room, such as a fireplace mantel or chair rail. Shades should end at the sill or bottom of the window opening or molding.

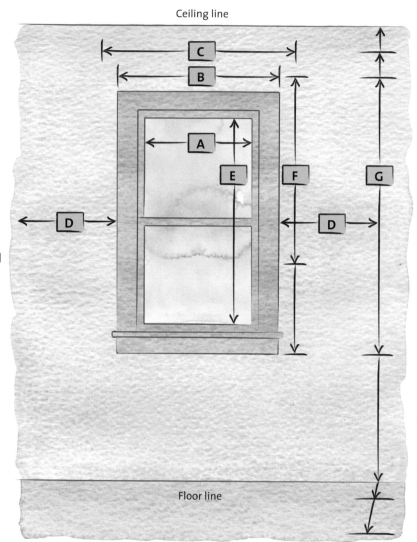

Ceiling line

Floor line

G: For drapery panels, mount treatments at the ceiling height or halfway between the window molding and ceiling, creating the illusion of height. If mounting just above the window, begin measuring 1 in. above the molding to ensure the panels cover the window properly. Panels can end ½ in. above the floor line or break or puddle on the floor. (See p. 150 for more on panel lengths.)

Specialty Windows

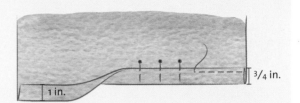

An arch-top window can be stylishly dressed simply by using one length of fabric and drapery tieback holders. Allowing the fabric to puddle gracefully on the floor eliminates the need for precise length measurements.

1. **MATERIALS:** Select a sheer or lace fabric 45 in. to 54 in. wide with an attractive selvage to avoid side hemming. Measure from the top of the arch to the floor and multiply by 2, then add 60 in. for draping and for the puddling effect. Divide this measurement by 36 in. to determine yardage required. Other items needed include three tieback holders, one 3-in.-dia. drapery ring with eye hook, one decorative tassel tieback, and household wire.

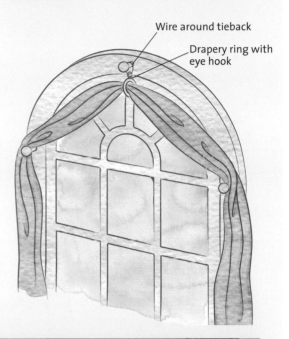

2. **CONSTRUCTION:** Cut the ends of the fabric square. To form double hems, press the ends under by 1 in. and fold over again by 1 in.; pin and press. Machine-stitch the hems in place by stitching ¾ in. in from each end.

3. **INSTALLATION:** Install holdbacks at the center of the window and at the sides below the arch. You can drape the fabric directly over the center holdback or insert the fabric panel through a drapery ring and use wire to secure the ring to the center holder. Drape the sides of the fabric over the side holders, arranging the fabric above into folds. Arrange the bottom edges in puddles on the floor. Tie a decorative tassel around the top tieback holder.

▲ **CONTRASTING CURVES** formed by this lace panel sweep across an arched window and provide an interesting overall design effect. Crystal bead trim outlines the edges of the lace, and decorative tassels add a defining touch of elegance above the arch.

▲ **THE STUNNING ARCHITECTURAL FEATURES** of this room, created by the shape of the walls and the ceiling, are enhanced by the arched windows, dressed with silk panels that have been draped open to reveal contrasting colors. A uniquely short pole holds each treatment in place and allows both sides of the fabric to show.

Adding Decorative Details

I T'S ALL IN THE DETAILS...a phrase that is particularly true
when it comes to window décor. Many times it's the finishing touches that set window treatments apart, turning them
into design statements within a room. Use your imagination when
looking for ways to enhance the appearance of otherwise ordinary
valances, shades, or drapery panels. You'll find inspiration everywhere—from a child's soccer or baseball gear to vintage trim you
found at a flea market. Craft and fabric stores are filled with
trimmings, and unusual ribbons, beads, tassels, buttons, and
appliqués may actually serve as the inspirational spark for artistic
window creations.

▶ THIS UNUSUAL TASSEL TRIM became a point of interest along the edges of
otherwise plain Roman shades. The tassel heights are staggered, softening the
linear feel in the room. The ecru color of the trim plays off the decorative knobs
adorning the ceiling's perimeter.

▶ AN ARTIST AT
HEART used thick
bullion trim as the
window treatment here,
allowing the glorious
seaside view to show.
The trim is swagged
across each window
and is tacked in place at
the edge of the ceiling.
Shells disguise the tacks.

◀ A CHILD'S DREAM BEDROOM was created here with auto-inspired décor. The highway carpet and racing car bed are artfully enhanced with the simple, black canvas valance wrapped around the windows, which sport a collection of luxury car appliqués.

Fabric Glue

You may be surprised to learn that many decorators use fabric glue to adhere trims to window treatments. Stitching can sometimes cause puckering, and this risk is eliminated by using glue. A hot glue gun also is effective for applying buttons, beads, and individual tassels. All of the glue methods dry quickly and form a lasting bond.

Select glue specially formulated for fabrics. Always test a sample on your materials first to check for show-through and get a feel for how much you'll need. Look for glues at your local fabric store or on-line notion's retailer (see "Resources" on p. 184).

When gluing, lay the treatment flat. If you're applying trim a considerable distance from the top or bottom edge of a treatment, measure and mark a chalkline at the desired point to use as the glue line. Tuck the trim end under by ½ in. Working in small sections, apply a line of glue over the chalkline. Lay the trim in place over the glue line and tuck the remaining trim end under by ½ in. Let the glue dry completely.

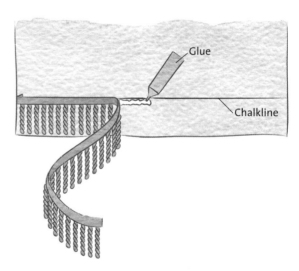

Glue

Chalkline

▶ USING FABRIC GLUE TO ADHERE BULLION TRIM across a lined drapery panel resulted in a pucker-free, smooth look across the panel. Stitching the trim would have proved difficult, as the cumbersome face and lining layers tend to shift during the process. Hot glue was used to attach the tassel cords to the points of the topper.

Rosettes

The rose-shaped ornaments you often see highlighting the center of a whimsical topper or the corners of a dramatic window dressing are called rosettes. Their interesting shape conveys a sense of dimension to a treatment, adding a distinct touch of style. A popular style, the Maltese cross rosette, is quickly formed with two layered bands of wide ribbon cinched together at the center with a button. Poufy fabric rosettes often are made from long strips of fabric gathered along one edge to form a flower-like effect. Placing the rosette slightly off the treatment at the top edge adds shape to the window.

► **THIS MALTESE CROSS ROSETTE** becomes a visual highlight at the center of this swag and jabot treatment. While you normally find swag styles in more formal settings, the delicate lace and ribbon trim along with the inventive rosette shape make this treatment perfectly at home in a child's room.

► **DECORATIVE DETAILS** such as rosettes and trim help to dress up this basic gathered valance. By styling the rosettes in the same fabric as the valance and draperies, the enhancement is subtle.

No-Sew Ribbon Banding

Enhancing the edges of a window treatment with ribbon can add striking flair to your project, and you can do so with ease when you take the no-sew approach. Fusible web, a product available in by-the-yard widths or in narrow rolls for hemming and applying trims, is often paper-backed so that you can make any ribbon or fabric fusible. The web melts when heated by an iron, forming a durable bond between materials. Here's how to apply ribbon quickly and stitch-free to the edge of an unlined window treatment:

MATERIALS: Satin or sheer fabric suitable for an unlined treatment; sewing pattern or your own design; grosgrain, satin, or organdy ribbon, $1/2$ in. to $3/4$ in. wide; one roll of paper-backed fusible web tape in a width similar to the ribbon.

HOW-TO: Fuse the tape to one side of the ribbon, following the manufacturer's instructions. Allow to cool completely and peel off the paper backing. Cut the fabric to the size and style desired for your window. Press all edges to the front side by $3/8$ in. Lay the fusible side of the ribbon over the folded edges, covering the raw edges completely. Fuse the ribbon in place, folding it at the corners for a mitered look. Tuck an extra piece of fusible web in the open fold of the mitered angles, turn the overlapping ends under, and fuse all in place.

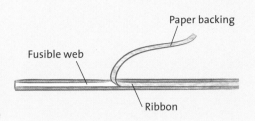

Paper backing

Fusible web

Ribbon

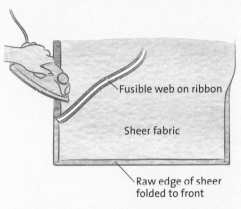

Fusible web on ribbon

Sheer fabric

Raw edge of sheer folded to front

▲ **STENCILED BIRDS** and mini grapevine wreaths anchor this one-of-a-kind window creation in place. The combination of ribbon banding and imaginative accessories can make any room personal and unique.

▲ **PENNANT-SHAPED TRIANGLES** in an assortment of striped and plaid fabrics offer simple style while the blinds take care of light exposure.

▲ **AN ELEGANT RIBBON** was fused in place along the inside and bottom edges of these store-bought drapery panels for a personal touch.

Customizing Ready-Mades

IF YOU'RE THINKING OF EXPLORING CUSTOM treatments for all of your windows, think again. The assortment of ready-to-hang drapery panels, window valances, and shades has grown tremendously over the past few years, and the fabric selection and quality makes them an attractive and time-saving option. Think of ways to inventively mount panels, such as placing two contrasting panels on one rod. Stitching coordinating panels into a new creation is another option, where a valance-like effect is formed at the top of a drape with trims defining the seam lines. Use your ingenuity to find ways to customize what's already out there; you'll save time and money in the process.

► COMBINING TWO SHIMMERING organdy panels on this bathroom window adds a Bohemian touch, especially when the outer layer is pulled up to reveal an embroidered design along the hemline. The panels were secured together with a decorative hand stitch to help keep them in place.

► TWO CONTRASTING PANELS mounted on a double curtain rod are tied back to one side of the window, revealing each color. A simple wood cornice neatly covers the rods and adds a customized feel to this inexpensive treatment.

Adapting Ready-Mades

Adding a color block of coordinating fabric to ready-made drapery panels can form a customized topper effect. Applying trim to the panels will create additional impact.

MATERIALS: For a pair of finished drapes, purchase four unlined, rod-pocket panels, all the same width. The two panels to be used for the bottom color blocks should measure the proper length for your window or doorway. The two panels for the upper block can be 54 in. long. For decorative trim, multiply the width of the panel by 2 and add 8 in. for one row of trim on each panel. Try adding a second row of trim in a contrasting color.

HOW-TO: For the upper block of fabric, use the 54-in.-long panels. The top rod pocket heading of each panel will be used as the top of the new drapes. Measure down from the top edge 20 in. and cut across the panels. Pin the top blocks to the bottom panels, aligning the top and side edges. Topstitch the panels together ½ in. from the bottom raw edge of the top color block. This raw edge will be hidden from view when trim is applied. Turn the panel over and cut away the top of the bottom panel ½ in. from the seam line. On the right side of the panel, machine-stitch or glue (see p. 173) the trim over the raw edge of the seam. Repeat to secure the second row of trim across the middle of the top color block.

MOUNTING: Install curtain rod hardware and hang the drapes. Pull the panels to the side with decorative tassel tiebacks if desired.

▲ **THIS CLEVER COMBINATION** of floral chintz and delicate lace gives a casual cottage feeling to this window. Blocks of the floral fabric were stitched to both sides of a lace panel, creating a valance effect that looks nice when viewed from the inside or outside.

▲ **THE BLEND OF COLOR,** fabric, and trim shown here lend eye-catching appeal to customized store-bought panels. Mounting the drapes on an interior doorway is a unique way to welcome passersby into the room beyond.

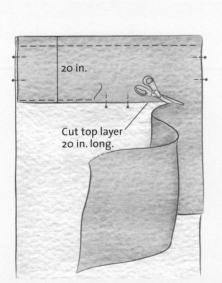

20 in.

Cut top layer 20 in. long.

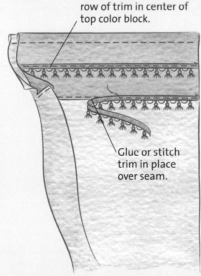

Glue or stitch additional row of trim in center of top color block.

Glue or stitch trim in place over seam.

▶ THESE PURCHASED
CHECKED DRAPES take on
a unique country theme with
bandanas looped over the
rod and threaded through
buttonholes along the top edges.
Cutting slits in the fabric instead
of making buttonholes also
works if you seal the raw edges
with purchased seam sealant.

▲ FRAMING A PURCHASED SHEER with a decorator
fabric pulls the colors in the room together while still
allowing light through the window. If the panel had
been made entirely from the blue toile fabric, the print
would have overwhelmed the setting.

▶ ENHANCING READY-MADE DRAPES with details like
attractive bandings along all edges adds personalized
style to this alcove. The matching ties securing the
treatment to the pole allow the fabric to fall in relaxed
folds that are tied back low and fall to the floor.

Creating Top-Edge Interest

The trick to drawing attention to the top edge of a panel is to select fabrics or trimmings that will serve to complement, not overpower, the treatment. Here, a purchased tulle panel in a little girl's room was creatively embellished with pastel bows.

1. **MATERIALS:** One white tulle or sheer panel with a rod pocket. The panel should fit the length of the window plus 20 in. For six bows, purchase contrasting tulle netting in three colors, ⅜ yd. each. To tie the panel back, purchase an additional ¼ yd. of one color. You will also need one 1-in. curtain rod sized to fit the width of the window plus 3 in.

2. **STITCHING PANEL:** To create a new 2-in. rod pocket with a 5-in. header or flap above it, cut the rod pocket off the top of the panel. Fold and press the top edge to the back of panel by 8 in. Press the raw edge under by ½ in. Pin the entire folded edge in place and stitch close to the fold. Stitch again 2 in. from the first stitching to form the rod pocket. Install the rod and panel over the window.

3. **BOWS:** Fold each color of tulle in half along the length of the fabric and cut along the fold. Tie strips into generous bows. Safety-pin or tack bows across the top of the treatment. Pull the panel to one side of the window and tie the remaining tulle around the panel. Thumbtack the tieback to the wall.

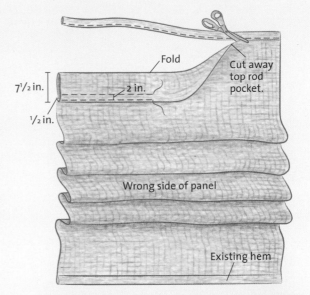

7½ in. · ½ in. · Fold · 2 in. · Cut away top rod pocket. · Wrong side of panel · Existing hem

▲ **WINDOW TOPPERS CAN BE MADE** from things other than fabric. Silk flowers and a wispy garden garland from a craft store are wired together to form a touch of nature along the top of this bathroom window.

◄ **FANCIFUL BOWS HIGHLIGHT** the frothy edges of a netting panel in this child's fairyland scene. The generous heading above the rod pocket mimics the fluttery feel of the butterflies; pastel bows finish the whimsical look.

Tools of the Trade

Cordless drill

Any job is easier if you have the right tools. Investing in a few handy items will help get jobs done quickly and professionally. Here are the top five must-haves for the do-it-yourself decorator.

1. **CORDLESS DRILL:** To drill pilot holes and install screws when mounting window treatments, buy a cordless, variable-speed model with ample 12-volt power. For convenience, the forward/reverse switch should be easy to reach and the drill should be lightweight and easy to hold.

2. **25-FT. TAPE MEASURE:** For precise window measurements, retractable tapes feature a lip on one end to grab the window molding and a locking system so you can stop to take the measurement. The 25-ft. length is perfect for other measuring jobs within the house, too.

25-ft. tape measure

3. **CORDLESS GLUE GUN:** Easy to use, the cordless glue gun heats up on a convenient stand. It is a perfect tool to help you glue on embellishments such as buttons, bows, ribbons, and appliqués.

4. **STAPLE GUN:** A staple gun is necessary if you plan to mount window treatments on boards. Look for a model that is comfortable to hold and loads easily. Purchase boxes of ⅜-in. and ½-in. staples to have on hand.

Cordless glue gun

5. **POWER SCREWDRIVER:** This tool can get into tight spots a drill may not be able to reach and is easy to use. Look for a model with 4.8 volts and a comfortable, pivoting handle that features auto-lock, so it can double as a traditional screwdriver.

Power screwdriver

Staple gun

Install It Right

Installing window treatments is relatively easy once you know the basics. Whether you're installing decorative knobs, curtain rods, poles, or board-mounted treatments, here's what you need to know about installing screws and wall anchors.

1. **FINDING THE STUD:** Wall studs are the wooden 2-in. by 4-in. or 2-in. by 6-in. boards that make up the framework of a house. Window treatments installed directly into studs are most secure since the screws mount into the wood. If there is no stud, anchors must be installed to secure the screw in the hollow area behind the drywall. To find a stud, knock on the wall to see if it sounds solid (stud) or hollow (no stud), or drill a small pilot hole into the wall, using a ⅛-in. drill bit to see if you hit wood.

2. **INSTALLING SCREWS INTO WOOD:** Use 1¼-in. screws or longer to reach the stud behind the drywall. If you're installing directly into wood molding, ¾-in. screws will work. Drill a small pilot hole first to make installing the screw easy.

3. **INSTALLING SCREWS INTO DRYWALL WITH ANCHORS:** There are many types of hollow wall anchors. The easiest types are self-drilling anchors. The plastic anchor screws into the wall first, and then the screw gets inserted into the anchor. For plastic molly or metal toggle bolts, drill a hole in the wall just big enough to fit the molly or bolt and insert it.

▶ **THESE READY-TO-HANG** drapery panels were banded to reflect the wall color and recut along the top edge into U-shaped scallops. The knobs were installed with screws featuring threads at both ends. One end screws into the decorative tieback knob, and the other end screws into the wall.

▲ **INSTALLING DRAPERY ROD HARDWARE** into wood molding requires ¾-in. screws that are secured directly into the wood. These lightweight drapery panels feature returns that wrap back to the wall at the ends, enclosing the window. The drape return is pinned or tacked to the wall or molding.

Resources

COMPUTER SOFTWARE

DreamDraper
Evan Marsh Designs, Inc.
P.O. Box 664
Bethlehem, PA 18016
(866) 56-DREAM
www.dreamdraper.com
Innovative tool to design
window treatments using
digital photos of your rooms.

FABRICS, TRIMS & WALL COVERINGS

Adaptive Textiles
319H Westtown Road
West Chester, PA 19382
(610) 918-9889
www.AdaptiveTextiles.com
Design your own one-of-a-kind
printed fabrics.

ADO International®
851 Simuel Road
Spartanburg, SC 29301
(800) 845-0918
www.ado-usa.com
Designer and manufacturer of
beautiful, fashionable fabrics.

Carole Fabrics®
P.O. Box 1436
Augusta, GA 3090
(800) 241-0920
www.carolefabrics.com
Manufacturer and distributor
of decorative fabrics and custom window treatments.

D'Kei Incorporated
P.O. Box 1570
Council Bluffs, IA 51502
(800) 535-3534
www.dkei.net
Designers and importers of
beautiful decorative trims
from around the world.

M&J Trimmings
1008 6th Avenue
New York, NY 10018
(800)-9-MJTRIM
www.mjtrim.com
The largest U.S. trim distributor, offering an unparalleled
selection of ribbons, embroi-
deries, fringes, and appliqués
from all over the world.

Wallies®
615 McCall Road
Manhattan, KS 66502
(800) 255-2762
www.wallies.com
Creatively inspired pre-pasted
paper cutouts, borders,
and murals in hundreds
of designs.

INTERIOR DESIGNERS

Bedeckers Interior Effects by
Kristine Gregory
P.O. Box 932
Midlothian, VA 23113
(804) 744-7645
bedeckers@comcast.net
Decorating services to create
a room that fits your lifestyle.

Creations by Corrine by
Corrine Zwiselsberger
corrine_z@hotmail.com
Specializing in residential
and commercial offices with
an emphasis on personalized
room design, custom window
treatments, and color coordi-
nation.

Interiors by Decorating Den®
8659 Commerce Drive
Easton, MD 21601
(800) 332-3367
www.DecoratingDen.com
Interior decorating and design
services with free in-home
consultation.

Interior Designer Home
Dressings by Holly Craiger
4018 Oak Forest Drive
Des Moines, Iowa 50312
(515) 633-0405
hhcraiger@aol.com
Full service interior design
firm specializing in window
treatments, from blinds to
drapery design.

Jamie Gibbs and Associates
Interior Designers and Land-
scape Architects
122 East 82nd Street
New York, NY 10028
212-717-6590
Branch offices in Indianapolis,
IN, and Amsterdam, NL.

Jody Porter Interiors
12 Blanchard Road
Easton, CT 06612
(203) 373-0127
Ilove2decor8@aol.com
Specializing in furniture placement, color and fabric selections, window treatments, and
all aspects of interior design.

Lisa's Distinctive Designs by
Lisa Hall
12 Soundview Drive
Easton, CT 06612
(203) 371-5009
lisa9039@sbcglobal.net
Complete decorating services
including room planning,
color selection, and window
treatment design.

The Window Dresser—Nika
Stewart
(800) 571-2468
www.WindowDresserNJ.com
Customized window designs
using unique style, creativity,
and attention to detail.

SEWING WEB SITES

Bernina, USA
2702 Prairie Lake Court
Aurora, IL 60504
(630) 978-2500
www.berninausa.com
Manufacturer of state-of-the-
art sewing, embroidery and
serger machines, and sewing
software systems.

The McCall Pattern Company
11 Penn Plaza
New York, NY 10001
www.McCallPattern.com
Producers of Butterick, Vogue,
and McCall's® Sewing Pat-
terns, including Home Dec In
A Sec® patterns (www.Home-
DecInASec.com) and Wallies
pre-pasted paper cutouts.

Nancy's Notions®
333 Beichl Avenue
Beaver Dam WI 53916
(800) 833-0690
www.NancysNotions.com
A leading catalog company
offering sewing, quilting, and
machine embroidery supplies.

OTT-LITE Technology®
Camille George
1214 W. Cass Street
Tampa, FL 33606
(813) 621-0058 ext. 364
Lighting products with low
glare, and naturally balanced
light that lets you see colors
and details easily.

Rowenta®
196 Boston Avenue
Medford, MA 0215
(781) 396-0600
www.rowentausa.com
Garment care expert and

manufacturer of high-performance irons, steamers, and ironing boards perfect for drapery making.

SHUTTERS, SHADES, BLINDS & FILM

B & W Manufacturing
263 Ambrogio Drive
Gurnee, IL 60031
(800) 858-2352
www.HorizonShades.com
Specializing in a unique variety of custom window coverings, featuring Shades of Elegance™ and Horizons™ soft treatments.

CP Films, Inc.
4210 The Great Road
Fieldale, VA 24089
(276) 627-3308
www.cpfilms.com
The largest producer of window film in the world for the residential, commercial, and automotive marketplace.

FUA Window Coverings®
LTD
899 South Castell Avenue
New Braunfels, TX 78130
(888) 857-9195
www.fuawindowcoverings.
com
A family-owned weaver and manufacturer of custom woven-wood window coverings since 1956.

Mastercraft Shutters®
3640 Weston Road, Unit 4
Toronto, Ontario M9L1W2
(800) 608-8837
www.mastercraftshutters.com
Offering window coverings to fit any budget or taste, with a strong commitment to quality and service.

Norman International®
12301 Hawkins Street
Santa Fe Springs, CA 90670
(866) 667-6228
www.normanshutters.com
A beautiful selection of custom shutters priced right, with the highest quality standards and backed by superior service.

Springs Window Fashions LP
7549 Graber Road
Middleton, WI 53562
(800) 221-6352
www.graberblinds.com
Manufacturer of Graber® window treatments, including blinds, shades, and drapery hardware sold through decorators and specialty retail dealers.

Vista Products®
1788 Barber Road
Sarasota, FL 34240
(800) 888-6680
www.vistaproducts.com
Precision shutters, wood and faux-wood blinds; pleated, cellular, and woven-wood shades; and panel track systems.

TOOLS & HARDWARE

Barbara K® Enterprises, Inc.
25 West 45th Street, 2nd Floor
New York, NY 10036
(800) 803-5657
www.barbarak.com
Offering a line of high-quality tools, toolkits, and accessories designed specifically for the do-it-yourself woman.

Lee Valley Tools Ltd.
P.O. Box 1780
Ogdensburg, NY 13669
(800) 871-8158
www.leevalley.com
A mail-order/retail supplier of cabinet hardware, woodworking, and gardening tools.

SOMFY® Systems, Inc.
47 Commerce Drive
Cranbury, NJ 08512
(800) 647-6639
www.somfysystems.com
A manufacturer and distributor of AC, DC, and battery-powered motors and electronic controls for every window-covering size and application.

TRADE ORGANIZATIONS

Home Sewing Association℠
P.O. Box 1312
Monroeville, PA 15146
(412) 372 5950
www.sewing.org
A non-profit organization promoting the home sewing industry. Web site features sewing projects and information regarding sewing teachers in your area.

Window Coverings
Association of America℠
(WCAA)
3350 McKelvey Road
Suite 202C
Bridgeton, MO 63044-2535
www.wcaa.org
A non-profit trade association dedicated to the retail window-coverings industry and to dealers, decorators, and workrooms.

DraperyPro
27281 Las Nieves
Mission Viejo, CA 92691-1010
www.DraperyPro.com
International Internet networking forum for workrooms, designers, educators, and industry vendors.

WINDOW TREATMENTS

The Silk Trading Co.®
5900 Blackwelder Street
Culver City, CA 90232
(310) 280-7500,
www.silktrading.com
Luxury textiles, draperies, and home furnishings available at showrooms across the country or from their website.

Home Dec In A Sec®
29 Soundview Drive
Easton, CT 06612
(866) 466 3352
www.HomeDecInASec.com
Quality custom window treatments available online. Interactive Web site instantly displays the latest window designs in over 150 fabrics. Fabrics and sewing patterns also available.

Credits

Chapter 1

p. 4: Photo © Samu Studios
p. 6: (top) Photo © Nancy Hill, design by Toni Gallagher Interior Design; (bottom) Photo © Samu Studios
p. 7: Photo © Eric Roth
p. 8: (top) Photo © Steve Vierra; (bottom) Photo © Eric Roth
p. 9: Photo © Brian Vanden Brink
p. 10: (top) Photo © 2006 Carolyn L. Bates/www.carolynlbates.com; (bottom) Photo © Mark Lohman
p. 11: (top & bottom) Photo © Mark Lohman
p. 12: (top) Photo © Samu Studios; (bottom) Photo © Alise O'Brien, design by Jamieson Design
p. 13: (top) Photo © Nancy Hill, design by Stirling Design Associates; (bottom) Photo © Ken Gutmaker
p. 14: (top) Photo © Melabee M. Miller, (bottom) Photo © Alise O'Brien, design by Sandra Ford/ Neva Moskowitz
p. 15: (top) Photo © Mark Lohman; (bottom) Photo © Tim Street-Porter
p. 16: Photo © 2006 Carolyn L. Bates/www.carolynlbates.com
p. 17: Photo © Eric Roth
p. 18: Photo © Melabee M. Miller
p. 19 (top) Photo © Jessie Walker; (left) Photo © Tria Giovan; (bottom right) Photo © Roger Turk
p. 20: Photo © Karen Ferguson, Harrison Design Associates
p. 21: Photo © Nancy Hill
p. 22: (top) Photo © Samu Studios; (bottom) Photo © Melabee M. Miller
p. 23: Photos courtesy Dream-Draper™
p. 24: (top) Photo © Nancy Hill; (bottom) Photo © Mark Lohman
p. 25: Photo © Eric Roth
p. 26: (top) Photo © Jessie Walker; (bottom) Photo © Mark Lohman
p. 27: (top) Photo © Tim Street-Porter; (bottom) Photo courtesy Decorating Den
p. 28: Photo © Eric Roth
p. 29: (top) Photo courtesy *Inspired House*, © The Taunton Press, Inc.; (left) Photo © Tria Giovan; (bottom right) Photo © Melabee M. Miller
p. 30: Photo © Mark Lohman
p. 31: (top) Photo © Jessie Walker;

(bottom) Photo © Roger Turk
p. 32: (top) Photo © Mark Lohman; (bottom) Photo © Roger Turk
p. 33: (top) Photo © Mark Lohman; (bottom) Photo © Tim Street-Porter
p. 34: Photo courtesy Carole Fabrics
p. 35: (top) Photo courtesy of The Silk Trading Co.; (top left & bottom) Photo © Tim Street-Porter
p. 36: (top) Photo © Sandy Agrafiotis; (bottom) Photo © Melabee M. Miller
p. 37: Photo © Chipper Hatter
p. 38: (top) Photo © Steve Vierra; (bottom) Photo © Melabee M. Miller
p. 39: (top right) Photo © Steve Vierra; (top left) Photo courtesy Carole Fabrics; (bottom) Photo © Lee Ann White, design by Betty Romberg

Chapter 2

p. 40: Photo © Jessie Walker
p. 42: (top) Photo © Jessie Walker; (bottom) Photo courtesy Vista Products
p. 43: (top) Photo © Alise O'Brien; (bottom) Photo © Jessie Walker
p. 44: (top) Photo © Steve Vierra; (bottom) Photo © Lee Ann White, design by Betty Romberg
p. 45: (top) Photo courtesy Vista Products; (middle) Photo © Steve Vierra; (bottom) Photo © Brian Vanden Brink
p. 46: (top right) Photo © Roger Turk; (top left) Photo © Samu Studios; (Bottom) Photo courtesy Norman Shutters
p. 47: (top) Photo courtesy Mastercraft Shutters; (bottom) Photo © Nancy Hill
p. 48: Photo courtesy Vista Products; (bottom) Photo © Mark Lohman
p. 49: Photo courtesy FUA Window Coverings
p. 50: (top) Photo © Steve Vierra; (left) Photo courtesy FUA Window Coverings; (bottom right) Photo © Mark Lohman
p. 51: (top) Photo © Chipper Hatter; (bottom) Photo © Tim Street-Porter; (left) Photo courtesy B & W Manufacturing
p. 52: (top) Photo © Mark Lohman;

(bottom) Photo © Chipper Hatter
p. 53: (right) Photo © Jessie Walker; (left) Photo © Tim Street-Porter
p. 54: (top) Photo © Mark Samu; (bottom) Photo courtesy FUA Window Coverings
p. 55: Photo courtesy FUA Window Coverings
p. 56: (top) Photo © Melabee M. Miller; (bottom) Photo courtesy Springs Window Fashions; (left) Photo © Brian Vanden Brink
p. 57: Photo © Melabee M. Miller
p. 58: (top & bottom left) Photo courtesy Springs Window Fashions; (bottom right) Photo © Steve Vierra
p. 59: (top & bottom right) Photo courtesy Springs Window Fashions; (center right) Photo courtesy B & W Manufacturing
p. 60: (top) Photo courtesy Springs Window Fashions; (bottom) Photo © Melabee M. Miller
p. 61: (top) Photo © Mark Lohman; (bottom) Photo © Jessie Walker
p. 62: Photo courtesy ADO USA
p. 63: (right & left) Photo © CP Films, Inc.

Chapter 3

p. 64: Photo © Mark Lohman
p. 66: Photo © Steve Vierra
p. 67: (top) Photo © Mark Lohman; (bottom) Photo © Brian Vanden Brink
p. 68: Photo © Jessie Walker
p. 69: (top right) Photo © Roger Turk; (bottom right) Photo © Eric Roth; (left) Photo © Samu Studios
p. 70: (top) Photo © Brian Vanden Brink; (bottom) Photo © Mark Lohman
p. 71: Photos © Samu Studios
p. 72: (top & bottom right) Photos © Mark Lohman; (left) Photo © Steve Vierra
p. 73: Photo © Brian Vanden Brink
p. 74: (top) Photo © Eric Roth; (bottom) Photo © Sandy Agrafiotis
p. 75: (top right) Photo © Steve Vierra; (top left) Photo courtesy Interiors by Decorating Den; (bottom) Photo © Steve Vierra
p. 76: (top) Photo © Melabee M. Miller, (bottom) Photos courtesy Interiors by Decorating Den
p. 77: (top) Photo © Timothy Kolk; (bottom) Photo © Chipper Hatter

p. 78: Photos © Samu Studios
p. 79: (top right) Photo © Tria Giovan; (bottom right) Photo © Eric Roth; (left) Photo courtesy Wallies
p. 80: (right) Photo © Jessie Walker; (left) Photo © Robert Perron
p. 81: (top right) Photo © Steve Vierra; (bottom right) Photo © Barry Halkin; (bottom left) Photo © davidduncanlivingston.com
p. 82: (top) Photo © Sandy Agrafiotis; (bottom) Photo © Nancy Hill, design by Hollis Interiors
p. 83: (top) Photo © Roger Turk; (bottom) Photo © Steve Vierra
p. 84: (top right) Photo © Jessie Walker; (bottom right) Photo © Melabee M. Miller; (bottom left) Photo © Nancy Hill
p. 85: (top) Photo © 2006 Carolyn L. Bates/www.carolynlbates.com (bottom) Photo © Barry Halkin
p. 86: Photo © Mark Lohman
p. 87: (top right) Photo © Chipper Hatter; (bottom right) Photo © Barry Halkin; (bottom left) Photo © Nancy Hill, design by Panache Interiors
p. 88: (top) Photo © Nancy Hill, design by Ann Davis/Robert David Architects; (bottom) Photo © davidduncanlivingston.com
p. 89: (top right) Photo © Nancy Hill, (top left) Photo © Eric Roth
p. 90: Photo © Eric Roth
p. 91: (top right) Photo © Nancy Hill, (bottom right) Photo © Robert Perron; (bottom left) Photo © Mark Lohman

Chapter 4

p. 92: Photo © Jessie Walker
p. 94: (top) Photo © Samu Studios; (bottom) Photo © Mark Lohman
p. 95: (top right) Photo © Samu Studios; (top left) Photo © Alise O'Brien, design by Joy Tribout
p. 96: Photo © Mark Lohman
p. 97: (top) Photo © Brian Vanden Brink; (bottom) Photo © Eric Roth
p. 98: Photo © Brian Vanden Brink
p. 99: (top left) Photo © Brian Vanden Brink; (top right and bottom) Photos © Jessie Walker
p. 100: (left) Photo © Mark Lohman; (right) Photo © Karen Ferguson
p. 101: (left) Photo © 2006 Carolyn L. Bates/www.carolynlbates.com;

(right) Photo © Eric Roth
p. 102: (left) Photo © Roger Turk; (top right) Photo © Steve Vierra; (bottom right) Photo © davidduncanlivingston.com
p. 103: (top) Photo © Eric Roth; (bottom) Photo © Nancy Hill
p. 104: Photo © Nancy Hill
p. 105: (top) Photo © Barry Halkin; (bottom) Photo © Brian Vanden Brink
p. 106: (top) Photo © Samu Studios; (bottom) Photo © Robert Perron
p. 107: (top) Photo © Eric Roth; (bottom) Brian Vanden Brink
p. 108: (top) Photo © Roger Turk; (bottom) Photo © Jessie Walker
p. 109: (top) Photo courtesy Interiors by Decorating Den; (bottom) Photo © Alise O'Brien, design by June Roesslein Interiors
p. 110: (top) Photo © Nancy Hill, design by Stirling Design Associates; (bottom) Photo © Jessie Walker
p. 111: (top) Photo © Mark Lohman, (bottom right) Photo © davidduncanlivingston.com; (bottom left) Photo © Chipper Hatter
p. 112: (top) Photo courtesy Lee Valley Tools; (bottom) Photo © Samu Studios
p. 113: (top right) Photo © Nancy Hill; (top left) Photo © Jessie Walker; (bottom) Photo © davidduncanlivingston.com

Chapter 5
p. 114 Photo © Jessie Walker
p. 116: (top) Photo © Tim Street; (bottom) Photo © Mark Lohman
p. 117: (top) Photo © Nancy Hill, design by Diane Burgoyne Interiors; (bottom) Photo © Jessie Walker
p. 118: (top) Photo © Chipper Hatter; (bottom) Photo © Tim Street-Porter
p. 119: (top and bottom right) Photos © Jessie Walker; (bottom left) Photo courtesy Carole Fabrics
p. 120: Photos © Samu Studios
p. 121: Photo © Eric Roth
p. 122: (top left) Photo © 2006 Carolyn L. Bates/www.carolynlbates.com; (top right) Photo © Samu Studios; (bottom) Photo © Tim Street-Porter
p. 123: Photo © Samu Studios
p. 124: (top) Photo © Steve Vierra;

(bottom) Photo © Brian Vanden Brink
p. 125: Photos courtesy Carole Fabrics
p. 126: (top) Photo © Steve Vierra; (bottom) Photo courtesy Carole Fabrics
p. 127: (top right) Photo © Nancy Hill; (bottom right) Photo courtesy The Silk Trading Co.; (bottom left) Photo © Eric Roth
p. 128: (top) Photo © Eric Roth; (bottom) Photo © Tria Giovan
p. 129: (top right and bottom right) Photos © Samu Studios; (bottom left) Photo © Ken Gutmaker
p. 130: (top) Photo © Nancy Hill; (bottom left) Photo © davidduncanlivingston.com; (bottom right) Photo © Mark Lohman
p. 131: (top) Photo © Mark Lohman; (bottom) Photo © Scot Zimmerman
p. 132: (top) Photo © Samu Studios; (bottom) Photo © Steve Vierra
p. 133: (top) Photo © 2006 Carolyn L. Bates/www.carolynlbates.com; (bottom) Photo © Eric Roth
p. 134: (top) Photo © Samu Studios; (bottom) Photo courtesy ADO USA
p. 135: (top) Photo © Jessie Walker; (bottom) Photo courtesy Carole Fabrics
p. 136: Photo © Jessie Walker
p. 137: (top left) Photo courtesy Interiors by Decorating Den; (bottom left) Photo © Steve Vierra; (right) Photo © Nancy Hill

Chapter 6
p. 138: Photo © Melabee M. Miller
p. 140: (top) Photo © Jamie Gibbs and Associates; (bottom) Photo © Tim Street-Porter
p. 141: (top) Photo © Samu Studios; (bottom) © Photo Chipper Hatter
p. 142: (top) Photo © Samu Studios; (bottom) Photo © Brian Vanden Brink
p. 143: (top) Photo © Samu Studios; (bottom) Photo © Brian Vanden Brink
p. 144: (top) Photo © Nancy Hill; (bottom) Photo © Mark Lohman
p. 145: Photo © Mark Lohman
p. 146: (top) Photo © Melabee M. Miller; (bottom) Photo © Samu Studios

p. 147: (top right) Photo © Melabee M. Miller; (bottom right) Photo © Jessie Walker; (bottom left) Photo © davidduncanlivingston.com
p. 148: (top) Photo © Brian Vanden Brink; (bottom right) Photo © Chipper Hatter; (bottom left) Photo © Melabee M. Miller
p. 149: Photo © Samu Studios
p. 150: (right) Photo © Roger Turk; (left) Photo © Brian Vanden Brink
p. 151: (right) Photo © Nancy Hill; (left) Photo © Tim Street-Porter
p. 152: (top right) Photo © Jessie Walker; (top left) Photo © Eric Roth; (bottom) Photo © Mark Lohman
p. 153: (top left) Photo © Mark Lohman; (top right, bottom right) Photos courtesy Spring Window Fashions
p. 154: (top) Photo © Tim Porter-Street; (bottom) Photo © Eric Roth
p. 155: (top right) Photo © davidduncanlivingston.com; top left) Photo © Mark Lohman; (bottom) Photo © Roger Turk
p. 156: (top right) Photo © Nancy Hill; (bottom right) Photo © Tria Giovan; (left) Photo © davidduncanlivingston.com
p. 157: (top right) Photo courtesy Interiors by Decorating Den; (top left) Photo © Steve Vierra; (bottom) Photo © Nancy Hill
p. 158: (top) Photo © Samu Studios; (bottom) Photo © Jessie Walker
p. 159: (top) Photo courtesy ADO USA; (bottom) Photo courtesy Carole Fabrics
p. 160: (top right) Photo © Alise O'Brien; (bottom right) Photo © Steve Vierra; (left) Photo © davidduncanlivingston.com
p. 161: (top) Photo © Scot Zimmerman; (bottom) Photo © Jessie Walker
p. 162: (top) Photo © Scot Zimmerman; (bottom) Photo © Robert Perron
p. 163: (top) Photo © Jessie Walker; (bottom) Photo © Mark Lohman
p. 164: (top) Photo © Samu Studios; (bottom) Photo © Nancy Hill
p. 165: (top right) Photo © Nancy Hill; (top left) Photo © 2006 Carolyn L. Bates/www.carolynlbates.com; (bottom) Photo courtesy ADO USA

Chapter 7
p. 167: Photos © Samu Studios
p. 168: (top) Photo © Jessie Walker; (bottom) Photo © Mark Lohman
p. 169: (top right) Photo courtesy Bernina USA; (bottom right) Photo courtesy Rowenta; (left) Photo courtesy Bernina USA, (bottom left) Photo courtesy Ott-lite
p. 171: (bottom left) Photo © Jamie Gibbs and Associates; (bottom right) Photo © Jessie Walker
p. 172: (top) Photo © Samu Studios; (bottom) Photo © Steve Vierra
p. 173: (top) Photo © Mark Lohman; (bottom) Photo © Chipper Hatter
p. 174: (top) Photo © Eric Roth; (bottom) Photo © Melabee M. Miller
p. 175: (left) Photo © Samu Studios; (middle) Photo © Nancy Hill; (right) Photo © Mark Lohman
p. 176: (top) Photo © 2006 Carolyn L. Bates/www.carolynlbates.com; (bottom) Photo © Nancy Hill, design by Diana Sawicki Interior Design
p. 177: Photos courtesy ADO USA
p. 178: (top) Photo © 2006 Carolyn L. Bates/www.carolynlbates.com; (bottom left) Photo © Samu Studios; (bottom right) Photo © Jessie Walker
p. 179: (right) Photo © Melabee M. Miller; (left) Photo © Alise O'Brien
p. 181: (top) Photo © Eric Roth; (bottom) Photo © Chipper Hatter

For More Great Design Ideas, Look for These and Other Taunton Press Books Wherever Books are Sold.

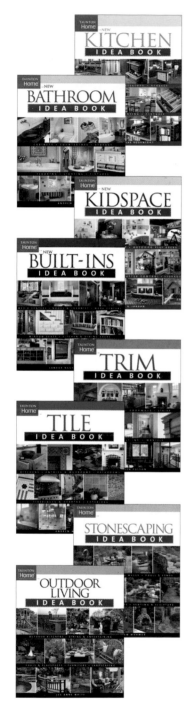

NEW KITCHEN IDEA BOOK
1-56158-693-5
Product #070773
$19.95 U.S./$27.95 Canada

NEW BATHROOM IDEA BOOK
1-56158-692-7
Product #070774
$19.95 U.S./$27.95 Canada

NEW KIDSPACE IDEA BOOK
1-56158-694-3
Product #070776
$19.95 U.S./$27.95 Canada

NEW BUILT-INS IDEA BOOK
1-56158-673-0
Product #070755
$19.95 U.S./$27.95 Canada

TRIM IDEA BOOK
1-56158-710-9
Product #070786
$19.95 U.S./$27.95 Canada

TILE IDEA BOOK
1-56158-709-5
Product #070785
$19.95 U.S./$27.95 Canada

STONESCAPING IDEA BOOK
1-56158-763-X
Product #070824
$14.95 U.S./$21.00 Canada

OUTDOOR LIVING IDEA BOOK
1-56158-757-5
Product #070820
$19.95 U.S./$27.95 Canada

ORGANIZING IDEA BOOK
1-56158-780-X
Product #070835
$14.95 U.S./$21.00 Canada

CURB APPEAL IDEA BOOK
1-56158-803-2
Product #070853
$19.95 U.S./$27.95 Canada

TAUNTON'S HOME STORAGE IDEA BOOK
1-56158-676-5
Product #070758
$19.95 U.S./$27.95 Canada

TAUNTON'S FAMILY HOME IDEA BOOK
1-56158-729-X
Product #070789
$19.95 U.S./$27.95 Canada

TAUNTON'S HOME WORKSPACE IDEA BOOK
ISBN 1-56158-701-X
Product #070783
$19.95 U.S./$27.95 Canada

BACKYARD IDEA BOOK
1-56158-667-6
Product #070749
$19.95 U.S./$27.95 Canada

POOL IDEA BOOK
1-56158-764-8
Product #070825
$19.95 U.S./$27.95 Canada

BABYSPACE IDEA BOOK
1-56158-799-0
Product #070857
$14.95 U.S./$21.00 Canada

DECORATING IDEA BOOK
1-56158-762-1
Product #070829
$24.95 U.S./$34.95 Canada

FOR MORE INFORMATION VISIT OUR WEBSITE AT www.taunton.com